Street party.
Planning
permission.
Booksho[p]

There aren't
many things
that bring
communities
together.

Waterstones

GRANTA

12 Addison Avenue, London WII 4QR | email editorial@granta.com
To subscribe go to www.granta.com, or call 845-267-3031 (toll-free 866-438-6150)
in the United States, 020 8955 7011 in the United Kingdom

ISSUE 124: SUMMER 2013

EDITOR	John Freeman
DEPUTY EDITOR	Ellah Allfrey
ARTISTIC DIRECTOR	Michael Salu
ASSOCIATE EDITOR	Patrick Ryan
ONLINE EDITOR	Ted Hodgkinson
EDITORIAL ASSISTANT	Yuka Igarashi
PUBLICITY	Saskia Vogel
ASSISTANT DESIGNER	Daniela Silva
FINANCE	Geoffrey Gordon, Morgan Graver, Craig Nicholson
MARKETING AND SUBSCRIPTIONS	David Robinson
SALES DIRECTOR	Brigid Macleod
SALES MANAGER	Sharon Murphy
TO ADVERTISE CONTACT	Kate Rochester, katerochester@granta.com
IT MANAGER	Mark Williams
PRODUCTION ASSOCIATE	Sarah Wasley
PROOFS	David Atkinson, Sarah Barlow, Katherine Fry, Jessica Rawlinson, Vimbai Shire
PUBLISHER	Sigrid Rausing
CONTRIBUTING EDITORS	Daniel Alarcón, Diana Athill, Peter Carey, Mohsin Hamid, Sophie Harrison, Isabel Hilton, Blake Morrison, John Ryle, Edmund White

2013

FICTION uncovered

GREAT WRITING TO DISCOVER
by eight of our favourite writers

THE HEART BROKE IN
JAMES MEEK
CANONGATE

BLACK BREAD WHITE BEER
NIVEN GOVINDEN
THE FRIDAY PROJECT, HARPERCOLLINS

THE COLOUR OF MILK
NELL LEYSHON
FIG TREE, PENGUIN

THE VILLAGE
NIKITA LALWANI
VIKING, PENGUIN

SECRECY
RUPERT THOMSON
GRANTA

ORKNEY
AMY SACKVILLE
GRANTA

ALL THE BEGGARS RIDING
LUCY CALDWELL
FABER & FABER

HOW I KILLED MARGARET THATCHER
ANTHONY CARTWRIGHT
TINDAL STREET PRESS, PROFILE

AVAILABLE FROM BOOKSTORES NOW

SELECTED BY OUR JUDGING PANEL

CHAIRED BY Louise Doughty **WITH** Sandeep Mahal Lynne Hatwell Courttia Newland

fictionuncovered.co.uk

Supported using public funding by
ARTS COUNCIL ENGLAND
LOTTERY FUNDED

CONTENTS

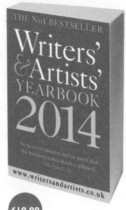

THE CAPTAIN

Rattawut Lapcharoensap

I was with Dora. We were in love. Things were cheap and plentiful and the money from the insurance was going to last us forever. We were in Thailand then Laos then Vietnam then Cambodia then Burma then Malaysia, though not necessarily in that particular order, I don't think. Cities, villages, provincial hamlets. The jungle, the sea, the mountains, the rivers. We looked at temples and saw traditional dancing and tried new foods and petted baby elephants and gave money to beggars and went to a crocodile farm and snorkelled with fishes and shopped in bazaars and haggled with the natives and then we went back to wherever we were staying that night – bungalow, hotel, resort, tent – to fuck with great enthusiastic happiness, to tremble in the tropical dew. Tourism as aphrodisiac; travel as foreplay. First World love, Third World magic. Sunsets, sunrises, stars up in the firmament, waves lapping at the shore. That kind of thing.

There were expats and backpackers and slum children and riverboat pilots and Vietnam War veterans. A middle-aged Scottish widow ran a private monkey sanctuary from her backyard in some generic suburb. Gibbons and macaques ate rice cakes from her hands, swung from her trees, hurled faecal discuses at night against the windows of her mansion. She said it was an expression of their trauma and abuse at the hands of poachers and smugglers. We thought it was an expression of something else, namely their hostility towards the woman and her suburban house. We lay in her spare bedroom and listened to the irregular thudding on her windows and that lunatic howling out in the dark and we wondered if the Scottish widow believed that we had needed rescuing too.

We bought pills from a handsome double amputee who got

around on a skateboard, propelling himself with his hands down the street as if he were a surfer heading out to catch a wave. He claimed to have learned how to speak English from listening to the BBC World Service and I believed him. He had perfect elocution. He counted out his pills and then counted out our money as if reading the news to the Empire, before paddling down the street into the subtropical night, the wheels of his skateboard trilling against the asphalt. He had one of the most beautiful faces I had ever seen. What a man, I thought, as he disappeared around the corner. What an inspiration. I wanted to be his friend. I wanted to know more about him. I wanted more of that elocution, more of that beautiful face. I wished that our relationship had been more than transactional, which was not an uncommon feeling for me at the time. Money was a solution that always became a problem. It was constantly bringing us into contact with such wonderful people only to immediately get in the way.

There was a masseuse who came back with us one night to a room overlooking some giant, filthy river. We flopped on the sheets while the river barges lowed beyond the pane and the masseuse attended to both of us simultaneously with startling ambidexterity. It both was and was not the kind of massage that either of us had expected. Pay attention, Dora turned to me and said. This is how you treat a woman, she said, closing her eyes. I take it all back, she said. This was a wonderful idea. She frowned and expelled a long whistling breath and pushed up her hips with yogic concentration and it occurred to me then that she might be serious – that I really should pay attention to what the masseuse was doing to my fiancée – but I was too distracted by the manual miracles being performed by the masseuse's other hand. See you next time, the masseuse said in English before she left, stuffing the money into a fanny pack and leaving us her business card, and afterwards Dora sat naked on a stool and read *Anna Karenina* out loud for a while and I remember thinking, yes, I remember thinking, all right, I remember looking up at the geckos suspended upside down on the ceiling, all of them regarding me with their beady and lidless and delicately jellied eyes, and I remember feeling at that moment as if I were in the warm, bright centre of heaven.

The Scottish widow, the double amputee, the ambidextrous masseuse: maybe that was one night instead of three. Or maybe that was three countries instead of one. But I suppose that it didn't matter then so it doesn't really matter now.

Listen, I said. I think I'm about to have an epiphany.

Be quiet, Dora said. I'm reading.

I'm serious, I said. I think I'm about to have a profound experience.

I know, Dora said. Didn't I tell you? This book is really very good.

No, I said. I'm not talking about the Tolstoy. I'm talking about me. I'm talking about us. I feel like we're on the cusp of something.

Stop, she said. You're being a jerk. I hate it when you interrupt me. And I hate it when you talk like that. I really don't like it at all.

Something's about to happen, I said.

Something's always about to happen, she said. Something just happened. That woman was incredible. We really should do that again. I feel like I'm still vibrating.

You think I'm joking, I said. You always think I'm joking. Why is that?

Because you're not a serious person, Dora said. Because neither of us has ever been a serious person. Look at us. This is not a serious situation. Sometimes I think that we're incapable of seriousness.

Hey, I said. That is not very nice.

Dora shrugged. She continued reading. Vronsky was doing something and Anna was doing something in response. I'd lost track of the story weeks ago, but didn't have the heart to tell Dora. I also hated the way she read aloud – nasal and uninflected and careless with her vowels – but I didn't have the heart to tell her that either. Tolstoy didn't stand a chance; she made him sound like a tone-deaf Appalachian with a sinus condition. But I had learned long ago that there were some things you best keep to yourself and that the keeping of those things was somehow important, was some important variety of love.

Have we been here before? I said. I feel like we've been here before.

Dora kept reading.

Enough, I said. No more Tolstoy. Let's talk.

No. She absent-mindedly worried her pubic hair and peered at me lying on the bed. Not now. We're just getting to the best part.

I'm trying to be serious now. Have we been here before?

Dora sighed, looked around the room.

I haven't been here before, she said. Nope. Not me. But maybe you have.

What do you mean?

What do I mean? Jesus. Do I really have to spell it out for you?

Yes, I said. Please. I'm lost without your explanations. That is one of the things that I mean when I say that I love you.

Well, Dora said. Her entire face had become a gigantic eyeball staring at me. Well, you're from here, you jerk.

It was clear that we were having an important disagreement about what was meant by the word 'here'. I rolled off the bed and went to stand by the window. Things were twinkling out there in the dark: stars, boats, headlights, buildings. The moon was glowing so bright, so close to my face, that I thought I could feel its refracted solar heat.

Phnom Penh? I said hopefully. Bangkok? Kuala Lumpur? Saigon? I really don't remember any more.

You're unbelievable. She put down the Tolstoy and started putting on her clothes. You make me sick sometimes, you really do.

The next morning Dora was gone. Surprise, surprise, I thought, but I was lying to myself a little, I wasn't surprised at all. She had taken half of the money but was kind enough to leave me a note. She also left me her engagement ring.

You were right, the note said in her characteristic scrawl. Something was about to happen. And now it has. I've had enough. I'm done. I'm getting off this sinking pleasure cruise. This is the way of disaster and doom. We are both of us too old for this shit. Good luck with everything. AND JESUS CHRIST FOR THE LOVE OF ALL THAT IS GOOD AND HOLY GET THEE TO A THERAPIST ASAP. You need help.

What did she know about good, about holy? I wondered. But I wasn't angry. I felt OK. I would have done the same. Good for you, I thought, reading and rereading her note. Good for you, Dora, I always knew you had it in you. I admired her sudden sense of initiative, her active participation in her fate. I would have left me too and had been wondering of late why Dora even bothered sticking around. To be honest, I was beginning to lose a little respect for Dora with each day she passed in my company. I was beginning to lose a little respect for myself, too, with each day that I passed with the same, but then again I really had little choice in the matter. I didn't have the luxury. I was the sinking pleasure cruise – as Dora had so wonderfully put it – or, at the very least, its hapless and inattentive captain. Not for me the lifeboat, the freezing Atlantic, the sharks in the water, the rescue team. I was going to have to go down with that fucker no matter what.

There was a maid vacuuming the floor. She kept running the nozzle over the same stretch of discoloured sideboard over and over again. She had headphones on and didn't seem to see me. I stood naked behind her for a while, waiting for her to notice me, feeling like a creep.

Hey, I said. Hey, hey.

She eventually turned around. She looked at me with a blank expression before resuming her vacuuming. My nudity seemed to make no impression upon her. I found myself looking down, running my hands over my body, to make sure that I hadn't accidentally clothed myself in the interim.

Hey, I said again, tapping her on the shoulder. Hey, will you please stop that? Some of us are trying to think over here.

No English, she said, waving her hands at me. I couldn't tell if it was an admission or an injunction. She glanced at my penis with mild irritation and then resumed her vacuuming again.

I got dressed and packed my bags. I walked down steps. There was an old man chain-smoking behind a counter who said that I owed him money. He held up my passport and said that he wouldn't give it back to me unless I gave him some money. I didn't know about any of that. I didn't know that I had given anybody my passport. But I was glad that somebody else had been taking care of it for me. And so I gave him some money and signed some papers and took back my passport and then stepped out into a city whose name I still couldn't seem to recall. I looked hopefully at the street signs, at the baroque fonts around me, as if I'd suddenly become some competent linguist, but this only made things worse. I really had no idea where I was, except that it was a sweltering Asian country with a graphically crazy alphabet. Dora had said that I was from here, I suddenly remembered, and I wondered what she'd meant by that. It didn't look like any place that I might be from; it only looked like a place that I would forever be going to.

Excuse me, I said to the first person that walked by, a beautiful woman in a business suit flanked by two handsome young children.

Please, I said. I think I need your help.

The woman shook her head and covered her children's eyes.

No! she said in English, drawing her children close and quickly pushing past me. No, no, no, no, no!

Later that morning I stumbled across a plaza before some gargantuan government building where people had gathered en masse. Hundreds of people were waving their arms and jumping up and down and then falling to the ground in unison while a certain strand of early-nineties techno blared in the upper air and a spry, muscular woman yelled at them from a makeshift stage. I thought it was a political rally at first and then I thought it might be a concert and then I thought it might be a religious tent revival of some kind, but one without any tents. I stationed myself beneath a tree on the plaza's perimeter and watched them for a while. I couldn't really understand what was happening in front of me. I was seeing things without seeing things. This was hardly a new sensation, of course, though what was new was that Dora wasn't there to make sense of it for me. What I'd said the previous evening was true – I was lost without her explanations – and I suddenly missed Dora with a force surprising even to myself. I thought I might begin to weep. This was hardly a new sensation either. It was such an old sensation, in fact, and such a persistent one, that I was afraid that it was becoming a condition. I was always, in those days, on the verge of unaccountable tears, in the grip of a blinding hysteria, full of strong feelings I couldn't name and, to make things worse, there was a man declaiming what I felt were some rather insensitive and unhelpful sentiments from the heavens, his smooth baritone voice issuing God-like from that thicket of throbbing techno bass lines concatenating in the atmosphere:

What is love?
Baby, don't hurt me
Don't hurt me
No more

No kidding, I thought, brushing my hands across my cheeks, but then somehow I suddenly figured it all out. I found that I didn't need Dora's help, after all. I was entirely capable of insights and revelations on my own and I sat there for a while marvelling at my new-found self-reliance as if I'd suddenly sprouted a useful extra limb. The people before me were exercising. They were doing aerobics. They were lifting their knees, clapping their hands, twirling around and punching the humid morning air, while the woman onstage led them by example and encouraged them all in a language I couldn't understand.

So I got up to join them. I felt I needed the exercise. Some self-improvement couldn't hurt, I thought. I left my bags under the tree and went to join the crowd: middle-aged housewives, elderly people, day labourers and maids and teenagers in shimmering sportswear, all moving in synchrony, faces flushed with happiness in their communal exertions. The sun rose slowly over the government building as if summoned by their aerobic supplications. I tried to follow the woman onstage, the people around me, but found that I couldn't keep up. I felt heavy, clumsy, neurologically scrambled.

I was always a quarter-step, a half-step, a full-step behind, and no sooner had I managed to catch up than I found myself immediately left behind once again by those around me, eating their awesome aerobic dust. I was making a spectacle of myself, I felt, despite my better intentions, and it occurred to me then, while I tried to keep up with the hale and healthy jigging around me, that this was not only a condition specific to the activity before me but also, in all probability, a more general problem in my life. People were snickering, glancing my way every so often with amusement and alarm. I was afraid that my efforts might be interpreted as disrespectfully ironic, culturally insensitive, and so I tried to arrange my sweaty face into a tableau of sincerity and concentration that would somehow argue against any such misinterpretation. A little girl in a purple velour tracksuit kept looking at me with aggressive condescension. She couldn't have been more than six or seven years old. She effortlessly executed the required manoeuvres, manoeuvres with which I was clearly having terrible difficulty, while managing to hold on her small and pretty and vindictive face a look of grave and obnoxious accusation. *Fuck off, little girl, mind your own business*, I would have mouthed in a former life, the kind of life that I'd been leading just a few days ago – just the previous day, even – but my new-found restraint in the face of her nymph condescension made me feel like things might really be changing after all. I smiled at her. I tried to ignore her, tried to focus on the task at hand, that task being a complicated series of alternating air punches that ended with a clap and a pirouette and a lift of each knee. I thought that Dora – wherever she was now – would have been proud of me.

I got into it, I really did, and as the sun crested over the top of the government building I felt that I was getting the hang of things. I felt like I was moulting out of my skin, sloughing something off. I was going native, in my way, losing myself in the crowd. I wanted to stay there in that plaza exercising with those people forever. But soon enough the music stopped and the woman onstage ceased yelling directives at us and the people around me began to towel off their faces and gather their bags and disperse. I stood there breathing heavily, arms akimbo, watching them leave, squinting at the preternatural glare of the new day's sun. MINISTRY OF THE INTERIOR, the sign on the government building declared in English, and I wondered what that meant. I wondered what that was. An old man humping a duffel bag smiled and gave me two thumbs up as he walked past, and I did the same. And I felt that between us had passed, for a split second, a wonderful mutual understanding, a miracle of reciprocity, and I wanted to embrace him in my happiness.

Humanism lives! I thought. That stuff is really real.

The woman onstage was standing before me, shaking a plastic bucket of money at me with great solemnity.

You have to pay, she said. Nothing is free.

Oh, I said. Oh, I see.

I gave her all of the change I had in my pockets. I would have given her more, to be honest. I felt that I couldn't give her enough, thank her enough. But when I looked in that bucket and saw the mess of currency inside I suddenly became distracted by the fact that the money seemed to be telling me exactly where I was.

Thailand? I said. Am I in Thailand?

The woman blinked at me.

I know it's a strange question, I said, laughing. But I really need to know.

She reached into the bucket and picked out a token of lint that I had accidentally deposited along with my change. She flicked it with a look of mild disgust, shook her head and walked away.

I went back to get my bags. But I couldn't seem to find them. I couldn't remember where I'd left them. I must have walked around the tree-lined boundaries of that plaza a dozen times that morning, looking for my bags. Men and women in tan and beige uniforms were streaming off city buses, walking across the plaza, entering the Ministry of the Interior. Oh well, I thought. Life can be like this sometimes. You get one thing only to lose everything else. I felt so good from the exercise that I decided I wasn't going to panic or cry about it. For a moment, I thought I saw Dora across the plaza, but when I approached her I saw that it was just a woman with a camera taking pictures of the place. I waved at her anyway. She frowned, took my picture and beat a hasty retreat.

After a while, I noticed a group of teenagers stationed beneath one of the trees, laughing at me, pointing in my direction. Every time I passed they seemed to fall silent, only to snicker and titter and laugh once more as soon as they thought I was out of earshot. I circumnavigated the plaza a few more times, looking for my bags, until I finally couldn't take it any more. I approached the teenagers – a girl and three boys, one of whom seemed to be doing a series of impressive one-handed pull-ups from a tree branch – and stood before them for a while.

Excuse me, I said. Do you guys speak English? Have you guys seen my bags? I'm looking for my bags.

Confusion briefly passed over their faces. They looked at one another, said some things in their language, laughed among themselves once more. The boy did a few more pull-ups and then lowered himself back down to the ground. The girl stood up, smiled at me and offered her hand. But when I reached out to take it I noticed that she wasn't interested in a handshake. She was pointing a switchblade at me. For a ludicrous moment I thought that she might be offering it to me but then I saw that her male colleagues had surrounded me now.

I had made a terrible mistake.

They weren't teenagers.

They were much older than I'd initially assumed.

We are very sorry, the woman said, smiling. Our English is not very good. We did not expect to have to use it. We did not think you were a tourist. We did not know you were a foreigner.

Oh, I said.

You are looking for your bags, yes? You would like them back?

Yes, I said. Do you have them?

We don't know, she said. Maybe we have them, maybe we don't.

We will have to see. Maybe you can come with us. Maybe we can look for your bags together.

She gently tapped the flat of her switchblade against my abdomen. One of the men put an arm around my shoulders. They all laughed artificially, patting me on the back and clapping their hands, as if I'd just told them all a very funny joke and was now revelling in their mirth and congratulation.

Oh, wow, I said.

We hope it's not an inconvenience, the woman said. Please come with us now. We will help you look for your bags.

I blinked. I found that I'd been holding my breath. All around us employees of the Ministry of the Interior continued to stream across the plaza.

We will put this away now. The woman closed her switchblade and pocketed it. We can see that it will not be necessary. We can see that you are a very nice person.

Wait, I said. Am I being mugged? Is that what's happening here?

No way, she said. Of course not. Why would you say that? You are hurting our feelings when you say that. We are friends now, yes? We are friends. We are friends and we are helping you look for your bags.

Please, I said.

Now it is our turn to ask some questions, she said. Is there anybody with you? Do you have a friend? Are you here with your family? Will anybody miss you? You are travelling alone, yes?

I had a fiancée, I said. But I don't know where she is. I lost her this morning.

How sad, she said. Perhaps we can help you look for her too. But we must ask you to be quiet now, she continued, nodding at her colleagues. We must ask you to come with us to our van. We can continue this interesting conversation there. Perhaps you can tell us about your fiancée. Don't look so worried, please. We are friends. We will help you find your bags.

And what if I say no? What if I don't go with you guys?

She smiled, said something to the men, and they all howled with laughter and patted me on the back and clapped their hands once more. One of them tousled my hair, tousled it so hard that I felt like he was checking the integrity of my neck.

In our culture, the woman said, we take friendship very seriously. Friendship in our country is a very serious business.

They shepherded me across the plaza, the woman leading the way while the men flanked me on all sides. One put his hand upon the small of my back; another whistled a shrill chromatic song as we walked; another kept swinging his right arm back and forth, as if he'd tweaked a muscle doing his pull-ups. The Ministry of Interior employees parted around us. I tried to make eye contact with one of them – with anybody, really – but nobody seemed to want to acknowledge us. We were just riff-raff wandering around the plaza on a workday morning. We were to be ignored. I looked around for the local police and nearly laughed out loud. Dora and I had spent so much time avoiding them in our travels and now they were nowhere to be seen. I thought about running. But, as if reading my mind, one of the men put me in a headlock, dragging me across the plaza, while the others laughed around me.

There was a minivan with tinted windows parked across from the plaza. One of the men opened the sliding door while another shoved me inside after the woman. I heard the door shut behind me, running along its rails and clicking home with a shuddering finality.

The woman patted the seat next to her.

We would like you to sit down next to us now.

My bags were in the seats behind her. It looked like somebody had disembowelled them.

Please, I said. Please, just let me go.

But we are friends, she said. We thought that we would help you look for your bags.

Well, I said. They're right *there*.

Somehow we were already moving into traffic. Somehow I found myself sitting between the woman and one of the men. The other two had gotten in the front seat. They all put on their seat belts. Somebody secured my lap belt for me. The sun was a dull disc through the tinted windows. A plaintive, down-tempo song was playing on the radio. The entire van smelled like potpourri.

Relax, the woman said. We are not going to hurt you.

She reached behind her, grabbed one of my T-shirts and handed it to her colleague beside me.

We are very sorry about this, she said, at which point her colleague wrapped the T-shirt around my eyes, tying it in a tight, painful knot at the back of my head.

The world became a darkness garrotting my eyeballs. Somebody gently rubbed one of my shoulders as if to console me. The men in the front seat laughed. One of them started whistling along to the song on the radio.

Are you comfortable? Is that too tight? Your comfort is important to us. Your comfort is our priority.

Please, I said into the darkness. I may have been crying, weeping into my unlaundered T-shirt, into the rancid stench of my own body odour.

Please, I'm begging you, I said.

You seem like good people, I said.

You don't have to cover my eyes, I said.

I wouldn't know about where we're going, I said. I don't even know where I am.

The van took so many abrupt and nauseating turns that I wondered if we might be driving in circles. At first, they all just sat there listening to my weeping as if I were a child having an unreasonable tantrum. I eventually managed to regain some composure and found, after a while, that in my blindness and panic I had become aware of my surroundings in a way I hadn't been in a very long time. I once was blind but now I see, I thought ridiculously, absurdly, the blindfold tight against my eyes. I became acutely aware of the street's modulating textures scrolling beneath my feet; the faintly chemical breeze luffing from the air-conditioning vents; the plaintive wailing of a woman's soft alto voice warbling on the radio; the spectral stench of something rotten and foul – my own bags, perhaps – for which the van's potpourri suddenly seemed a comically inadequate mask; the dull throbbing of the twice-obscured sun imperceptibly rotating around the van; that chalky, adrenal taste coating my tongue.

The four of them had been engaged for quite some time in a heated exchange. They were having a conversation about me, I realized after a while. In the thicket of that language I thought I heard them uttering my name.

They were saying my name in a way that I hadn't heard in a long time. They said it in a way that only my parents, I realized, had been able to say it.

I can give you money, I said. Just take me to a bank. Just take me to an ATM. I can make you rich.

We have some good news. We have found your wallet, the woman said. But we have a few important questions for you.

OK.

You are American, yes?

Yes, I said. Yes, I am.

You are telling us the truth?

Yes, I said. Far as I know.

But you do not have an American name.

I felt myself nodding. This was not the time, I thought, for a discussion about semantics, about politics.

Your name, she said, is not a foreign name. We are a little surprised, to be honest. We are a little worried. We are worried that you are lying to us about who you are. We hope that this is not the case. Friends should not lie to each other.

Friends shouldn't blindfold each other either, I said. A blindfold is not the best way to start a friendship.

Ha! You are very funny! the woman said. We can see that you have a big sense of humour.

But we must know about your name, she went on. Please explain. Let's get acquainted.

So this is Thailand, I thought. So that's what Dora had meant.

But I didn't think those things at all. I had said them aloud instead. I began to laugh. I once was lost but now I'm found, I thought, and the irony of it all only redoubled my laughter; I felt that I was practically choking on it.

A long expressive silence ensued. Somebody switched off the radio. The muffled noise of the traffic outside issued around us as if we were underwater. I felt an imperceptible shift in the air, a darkening of the van's collective mood.

Yes, the woman said. Yes, you are in Thailand. Welcome to our beautiful country.

My parents were from here, I said.

How interesting.

But I was born in America, I said. I have lived in America all of my life.

How interesting, the woman said again. And then: We must say that we do not like to make friends with Americans. Americans, we have found, can be very troublesome friends.

Another discussion ensued between them. The van stopped and lurched and stopped and lurched again. I found that I could abate the pressure around my head if I squinted hard against the blindfold. I was relaxing a little. I felt, in some strange way, that the laughter and the talk had done me good.

We must ask you to stop smiling now.

I felt the switchblade hard and cold under my shirt, against my abdomen.

We must ask you to respect the seriousness of our friendship, the woman continued. You will answer a few more questions, please.

OK.

Where is your mother? Where is your father?

They're gone, I said.

Gone?

Dead, I said.

We are very sorry to hear that, she said.

Me too, I said.

And you are here to collect your inheritance? You are here to pay your respects? You have come to visit the homeland of your parents?

I suppose, I said. I suppose that's why we came here. I suppose that was the intention. But we got a little – well, we may have gotten a little distracted.

We?

Me and my fiancée.

The one you misplaced?

Yes, I said. The one I misplaced. That's actually a wonderful way of putting it.

You will be quiet now, she said.

OK.

Silence, please.

Sure.

You will shut your mouth, she said. You will shut your mouth or we will have to shut it for you.

The van stopped and they finally took off the blindfold. We were in an anonymous bedroom community far from the city centre. They ushered me out of the van and we stood before some town-house row while one of the men unlocked the front gate. A mangy stray dog was licking its wounds under the shade of the property wall, eyeing us piratically with its one good eye every so often, flies orbiting its scarred and spotted flanks. A woman cycled by with a basket full of fresh produce. She smiled and rang her bicycle bell as she passed. The men waved at her and said something in response, pointed at me as if I might be a friend or a relative visiting from out of town, and the woman cycled away.

Welcome to our home, the woman said.

Once inside, the men turned on a television and slumped onto an old leather couch. A soccer match was on. They groaned at the scoreline, lit cigarettes, leaned forward on their knees, waving their hands every so often in exasperation.

Move, please, the woman said, nudging me in the back.

I went up a set of dark stairs, the woman close behind me.

Which room would you like? the woman said, as we stood on the second-floor landing before several gaping doors. You may choose.

Please, I said. Just let me go. I swear I won't say a word to anybody about this.

How about this one? she said, pointing at one of the rooms. There is a nice bed inside. It also has a nice view. It is the nicest room in the house. We think that you will find it very comfortable.

Please, I said again, but the woman had shoved me inside and closed the door behind me. I heard her locking the door from the other side, heard her footsteps going back down the stairs.

The room was empty save for a small bed. The windows were barred.

I tried the door handle to no avail.

I started knocking on the door.

Please, I said, knocking with greater and greater force. Please, I'll do anything you ask! What are you going to do to me?

From downstairs came the sound of the men cheering and clapping at the game, at the desperation in my voice.

You will stop that, please, I heard the woman say eventually. You will calm down. If you are not satisfied with your room, you do not have to shout.

What are you going to do to me? What is this about? Where am I? And why won't you just let me go?

We thought that we already told you, the woman said. We thought we made ourselves perfectly clear.

I stood with my head against the door listening to her voice, to the woman's strange, untraceable accent talking on the other side of the wood, and it occurred to me then that I might be dead, that this is probably what happened to souls such as mine in the afterlife. No harp-bearing angels. No pearly, luminescent gates. Just a small, dark room in some generic suburban development and a lunatic woman talking in plural pronouns.

Thank you, the woman said. Thank you for calming down. Thank you for your understanding.

I don't understand, I said. I don't understand what this is about.

We want you to be comfortable, she said. We want to be your friends.

The woman went back downstairs. I moved to the window after a while and looked out onto the street before the town-house row. Nobody was out there save for that mangy dog now dragging herself across the asphalt. I lay on the bed, listening to the sounds of my captors' voices below me. Time somehow passed, though it didn't seem to pass at all. I wondered what Dora was doing, where she was, whether or not she was thinking of me.

I must have fallen asleep. I woke to the woman's voice at the door, to the evening sky beyond the window rioting with colour.

We are hungry and we were wondering if you were too.

She opened the door. She was holding that switchblade again, twirling it in her hand as if she might be some circus performer. One of the men dragged me to my feet.

Let's go eat, she said, smiling. What kind of cuisine do you like? Would you like some Japanese food? We have never eaten Japanese food. We would like to try.

So into the van again. So into that garrotting darkness. They blindfolded me once more and we drove in silence for a while.

We have more good news, the woman said. We have finally found your bags! There was quite a lot of money in your bags. We have put it in a safe place for you.

I didn't say anything.

You should be polite, she said. You should thank us for finding your bags and your money.

Have we done something to make you angry? she continued, when I didn't respond again. Have we done something to offend you? Friends should talk to each other.

Do you guys do this a lot? I finally asked. Rob and abduct people?

Who is robbing? Who is abducting? she said. Do we have a gun to your head? We do not have a gun to your head. We have a gun, yes, but we do not have it to your head.

We also found a beautiful ring in your bags, she continued. We will give it back to you now. It is a diamond ring, yes? Your fiancée's ring? We do not understand why she would leave a good man like you, a man who would give her such a good ring. But we will give it to you now. We will do this to show you that we are not robbers, that we are your friends.

I felt her pressing the ring into my hands, closing my fingers around it. I didn't know what to do with it. After a while, I just slipped it onto my finger, as if I might now be engaged to myself.

See? she said. We are friends.

I really wish you would stop saying that, I said.

We have also found your ATM card, she continued. This is another piece of good news for you.

The van had stopped moving.

Please tell us the code, she said. We would like to borrow some money from you now.

I told her. Somebody exited the van and returned after a few minutes.

Thank you, the woman said. You are being very good. You are being a very nice, a very generous American.

You're welcome, I said, and I sort of meant it, I didn't care about the money any more, had never cared about it in the first place.

The van started moving again.

Just drop me off, I said. Just stop the van. I'll find my way home. I swear I won't make trouble for any of you.

But we are just becoming acquainted, the woman said.

Somebody turned on the radio. The men began to hum along to a song.

Can I ask you a question? I said after a while. Am I dead?

The woman laughed.

No, she said. You are not dead. You are alive. You are alive and we are now at a Japanese restaurant.

This went on for a quite a while.

Over the next few days it seemed like we ate at all the best restaurants in town. Just my luck, it turned out that I'd been abducted by a bunch of gourmands. They really knew how to live, those lunatics. Japanese, French, Korean, Ethiopian, Chinese, you name it. We ate it all. We sat in those restaurants like a bunch of siblings while under our table the woman played with her switchblade and the three men ordered everything on the menu, stuffing their faces and talking in loud, enthusiastic tones, while an endless parade of entrées materialized before us as if conjured by so many celestial hands. At a dim sum palace the waiters put a candle in an egg custard and sang me happy birthday and when I blew out the candle my captors all applauded and congratulated me on the fake milestone.

Happy birthday to our very good friend, the woman said.

By that point so many waiters at so many restaurants had sung me happy birthday that I was beginning to get a little annoyed. I stared at the egg custard and told her it wasn't my birthday and she told me to shut up. She produced my passport and showed it to me and I saw that she was right – that it actually was my birthday that day – and I couldn't tell if I was touched or afraid for my life. A lot of time seemed to pass like that. When I needed to go to the bathroom, one of the men always accompanied me, as if we might be teenaged girls going to gossip, or lovers heading for a quick, dirty tryst. The men usually checked their hair and their complexion in the mirror while I went about my business, although once – in a shiny marble bathroom in some Italian place – my escort suddenly produced a handgun, pointed it at me and urged me to wash my hands, as if my hygiene were a matter of grave importance.

They were having a pretty good time.

Now and again we went back to the town house and I was made to sit in that horrible room. But mostly we were out in the van. Mostly I just sat blindfolded while they drove around looking for new and ingenious ways to spend my inheritance. We went to restaurants and bars, department stores and hardware emporiums. We went to open-air markets and furniture warehouses. We went to several shopping malls and they all bought themselves a new wardrobe, a computer, a sound system, houseplants, cookware, books, DVDs. The men and I sat around in the waiting area of a department-store dressing room while the woman tried on business suits, and after she was done we all headed up a set of escalators to the mall cineplex to watch an American action movie.

It was a relief to be sitting in the darkness of that theatre. I could almost forget about what was happening to me. I wanted that terrible movie to go on forever. I wanted the alien apocalypse prolonged indefinitely, the world to keep on exploding, remain mired forever in its doomsday despair, so that when the aliens were vanquished and the world was invariably saved and the house lights went up I burst into tears.

There, there, the woman said, patting me on the back and offering me a handkerchief. All around us our fellow moviegoers looked on in bewilderment as they made their way out of the theatre. Don't cry, she said. It's just a movie. If you keep crying, we're going to leave you in the van next time.

What are you going to do to me? I said. Are you going to kill me?

Don't be hysterical, she said. We are not going to kill you. We are going to drop you off at the airport. Your flight leaves in a few days, yes?

I don't know, I said. I don't know about any of that.

It leaves in a few days, she said. There was a plane ticket in your bags.

Later that night we ended up at a nightclub. I was pretty sure that Dora and I had been to that nightclub before. And as I sat between my captors in a leather booth – drink after drink after drink appearing before us – it occurred to me that everything that had happened to me once was somehow happening all over again. First time tragedy, second time farce, and all that ridiculous stuff. Though perhaps that wasn't quite right, I thought. Perhaps it was actually the other way around.

They told me to drink and I drank. They told me to smoke and I smoked. The men headed out to the dance floor and the woman urged me to do the same. But I told her I didn't feel like dancing.

You will dance, she said. You will get up and dance with us now.

She grabbed me by the hand and led me out to the dance floor. The crowd around us seemed a single epileptic organism heaving to the music, to the lights flashing and sweeping around us. We found the men out there and they all smiled and yelled at us with great happiness, waving their arms to the music, welcoming us to their circle. The woman began to shimmy her shoulders and move her hips and twirl her hands in the light-speckled air. We must have seemed at that moment like so many friends out on the town for the night, and I found myself paralysed among them, overcome with a sense of my own smallness, feeling myself as a still, unmoving point around which the crowd seemed to convulse and to rotate, watching the faces of the dancers around me appearing and disappearing under the fitfully strobing lights. Here I was, desperate for help, afraid for my life, and yet nobody around me could detect any of it. And it occurred to me then that under the cloak of everyday life – a birthday dinner, a shopping excursion, a trip to the cinema, a night out on the town – this other thing was going on in plain sight, had perhaps always been going on, was perhaps going on with so many other people on this dance floor, and that there was no alibi quite so perfect as an ordinary good time.

Dance! The woman had grabbed my hand, was swinging it in time to the music, the floorboards thrumming beneath us. Dance, American, dance!

I decided then that I would try to walk away. I would just put one foot in front of the other and walk away from them all. This was all a colossal bluff, I thought. It was all a terrible joke, a joke for which I was the unfortunate punchline. What were they going to do? Stab me on the dance floor? Shoot me in front of all of these people? Murder me in a crowded nightclub? I eyed the exit. I tried to gather my wits, my strength, my courage, all the rest. I began to push my way past the woman, past the men, slowly negotiating my way through the crowd.

Where are you going?

A large white man was grinding himself against a small Asian woman. He shot me a look of disgust when I tried to shoulder my way past him.

Please, I said to the man. Please, you have to help me.

Keep moving, the man said in a Germanic accent, pulling the woman closer, as if I'd tried to steal his dance partner. Help yourself.

You don't understand, I said. I've been abducted. They're coming after me.

The man rolled his eyes and pulled his partner closer.

Where are you going?

I kept walking. I didn't look back to see what was happening, to see if they were following me, though I heard the woman's insistent voice calling after me beneath the clamour of the music. I kept walking through those pinpricks of swirling light, towards the exit, towards whatever freedom awaited me beyond that door. But when I finally got to the edge of the dance floor I found the three men waiting for me.

Somebody kicked my feet out from under me. I felt myself falling to the hard, sticky floor. One of them leaned over me and pretended to pick me up – to help up his drunk and hapless friend – but he was actually slapping me repeatedly, his blows landing flush against my cheeks in time to the rhythm of the music. The others stood around with looks of grave concern, as if I might be an embarrassing friend – the kind of friend who habitually caused such unseemly and disastrous scenes – the sort of person who always turned a good time into a bad one – while the man sat there straddling my chest and slapped me around in the dark, his blows landing swift and imperious against my cheeks. I lay there receiving the man's blows and I didn't know whether to laugh or to cry or to howl out in pain, for I felt that I was a little drunk, actually, and I knew that I had been that person, that embarrassing friend, and I suddenly missed everybody then – Dora and my parents and everybody that I had ever loved – and I wanted very badly to see them all again.

They picked me up and carried me out of the nightclub, slung between two of the men, my face a throbbing and insensate thing.

We must say that we are very disappointed, the woman said when we all got into the van again. Very, very disappointed.

I'm sorry, I said. I had to try.

What terrible manners, she said, shaking her head. What is it with you Americans? We were having a perfectly wonderful time.

I really don't know how to answer that question, I said.

We should punish you, she said.

Please, I said.

We should punish you for your misbehaviour, she said.

That won't be necessary, I said.

We should teach you a lesson.

You really don't have to do that, I said. Lesson learned.

Who knows what that lesson was? Who knows what I managed to learn from it all? Who learns anything from anybody any more? I didn't know then and I still don't know now.

But three days later they dropped me off at the airport. They parked the van and carried my bags to the kerb and then they each embraced me as if they were friends bidding me bon voyage. The woman handed over my passport and my plane ticket and then she hugged me for a while, as if she might be my girlfriend, and I thought that there might even be tears in her eyes.

Thank you for everything, she said. Thank you and good luck. We hope that you've enjoyed your visit to our beautiful country.

By that point they'd taken me for all that I had. They'd emptied my bank account, maxed out my credit cards, and one of the men had even taken most of my clothes. I stood there with the woman's arms around my waist, with her face looking up at mine, strangely afraid that she might try to kiss me. I simply didn't know what to say. I suppose that I wanted to thank her too – thank her for sparing my life, or something, though I don't think they ever intended to kill me – but by then she'd disappeared into the van and I soon lost them in the throng of kerbside vehicles pulling away from the terminal, heading back into the city.

And so I had my freedom again, in a way.

There was a policeman directing traffic nearby. It occurred to me that I should talk to him, maybe report the ordeal. But I didn't know what to say, didn't know how I would ever explain any of it, and besides I'd always hated talking to cops. Those people had never done anything for me.

I found Dora sitting at the gate, reading *Anna Karenina*. She was wrapped in a sarong of some kind. She had a suntan. She had a new haircut. She'd never looked so beautiful to me as she did then.

I walked up to her and waited for her to notice me.

How does that thing end? I eventually asked.

She looked up at me for a while, blinking.

Poorly, of course, she said. Wonderfully, but poorly.

I wish you hadn't left me like that, I said.

She shrugged.

I missed you, I said. I really did.

Sure, she said. That was the point.

I love you, Dora, I said.

How nice, she said, laughing. Good for you.

And so I got down on my knees.

And so I took off the ring and asked Dora to marry me again.

What happened to your face? she said afterwards, the applause of our fellow passengers dying down around us.

Are you being serious now? I said, brushing the tears from my eyes. Do you really want to know? For some reason, I don't think that you really want to know.

You're right, Dora said. She turned back to the novel. I don't. ■

ARVON

**GROW
YOUR
OWN**

RESIDENTIAL
CREATIVE WRITING
COURSES 2013

Come to an Arvon
centre, and grow your
own story. Fiction.
Non-fiction. Poetry.
Drama. Songwriting.
Comedy. Memoir. Text
and image. For children.
For radio. For film and
TV. You name it. All
varieties are here. We
also have a programme
of courses for schools
and community groups.

Find out more, support
our work, apply for a
grant to help with fees,
or book a course at:

www.arvon.org

@arvonfoundation

Supported using public funding
by Arts Council England

THE PERFECT LAST DAY OF MR SENGUPTA

Siddhartha Mukherjee

In November 2007, I travelled from Boston to New Delhi to visit my parents. It was an unseasonably cold week. A dense fog from the northern mountains had poured into the caul of the city and sat, soupy and unmoving, for days on end. Connaught Place, the epicentre of the city's commercial activity, was deserted until noon, when an occasional shard of sunlight parted the fog – but the late afternoon sank back again into the darkness, and the streets went dead. The migratory ducks from Siberia floated in the pond of the nearby zoo looking sullen and miserable, like duped tourists.

One morning, tired of being confined at home, I went to visit my cousin's wife who is a social worker at the All India Institute of Medical Sciences. The institute – AIIMS – is a government hospital a few miles from my parents' house.

Nothing prepares an outsider for the cavernous waiting room of the hospital. The word that comes to mind is 'post-apocalyptic', although the 'post' may be superfluous: the place is simply apocalyptic. The waiting room resembles a railway platform or a refugee camp – a vast, open, neon-lit space crammed with men, women and children sprawled out on the concrete floor with beds, cots, rags, medical records, X-rays, papers, documents and food stacked in between. The patients are like supplicants on a pilgrimage; they have arrived from all parts of the country and set up camp here, waiting to be seen by the doctors on call. In fact, the colloquial term used for this clinical encounter is *darshan* – which means 'vision' or 'appearance', as in a transient vision of a temple shrine, or of a god.

As with any pilgrimage, it is the labour of waiting, not its consummation, that defines the *darshan*. There is a formal system of appointment times, I think, handed out on chits of paper, but a secret economy has grown out of them: the chits are traded freely on the open market of the floor, like money, bought and sold to those who wish to pay for earlier appointments. Space, too, has its curious economy. The stairwell to the side, with raised steps, has a special premium, since it creates a makeshift bed for patients to lie on while their relatives crowd the lower steps, holding their hands and fanning their faces.

The doctors and nurses are overwhelmed, but they try their best. Once called into the examining room, patients have about seven minutes – maximum – to state their case, to be seen and examined, to be handed a diagnosis and, if necessary, to be admitted to the wards upstairs for treatment.

My cousin's wife works for a non-governmental organization (an NGO, as they call it here) that helps indigent children with cancer. Her NGO provides money for medicines and chemotherapy. It finds housing for the families that are detained in the city for weeks or months – a 'servant's' room in the back of the house, or an extra bedroom donated by a friend. It's a near-impossible task to pull off in this wary, suspicious city, but the enormity of finding living arrangements is dwarfed by the other aspects of her job: explaining the bizarre nuances of cancer treatment to the bewildered children and their parents, or providing palliative care and support to those who face pain and death. The last time we spoke, she told me why she loves her work: 'I love seeing the faces,' she said. But as I watch her, surrounded in a thicket of men and women thrusting letters, medical forms, housing requests and hospital receipts at her, I cannot help think that what she really looks at all day are arms and fingers.

There is no way she can leave this crowd to walk around with me, as promised – but then, as often happens in India, a man appears out of nowhere and offers to take me through the hospital. He introduces himself as Jairam. I don't know him, and he is clearly not a doctor, but he seems to know my cousin's wife, and bears an air of authority around the waiting room. I agree to accompany him.

The visit begins conventionally enough. We are in the upstairs wards, and he is seemingly friendly with some of the doctors and nurses, and introduces me as a fellow oncologist, a visitor from Boston. The doctors chat with me and ask me questions about my practice. Occasionally, they describe a case in detail – a child with a rare eye tumour, for instance, or a young girl with a leukaemia that has relapsed, strangely, in her skin – but the patients are in their rooms, out of earshot, and the names are mentioned so fleetingly that they may as well be anonymous.

We move down to the next floor, and Jairam stops in front of a room and asks me a favour: would I mind saying hello to a friend's father who is in a room by himself?

Before I can answer, he has already ushered me into a small ward-room on the fifth floor, with a slit-like window. The room is suffused with the smell of disinfectant and soap. There is a man wrapped in a thin grey blanket on the bed. His wife, sitting by his side, introduces him as Madhav Sengupta.

'Kidney cancer,' she says, motioning to the bed. 'It's in his bones as well, and he can't seem to shake the pain.'

Jairam turns to me. 'It's a terminal case. Very advanced.' He lowers his voice to a whisper: 'Mr Sengupta has been in the hospital for three weeks. There's nothing to do. He wants to die, but they won't let him.'

I make a subtle motion to protest and get up. Even by the standards seemingly acceptable in this public hospital, the violation of his privacy is astounding. This is not my patient. I hardly know this family. The information, and the man's pain, are already overwhelming. I want to leave.

But there is no way out. It is as if the doors have closed invisibly behind me. 'Perhaps this doctor can help,' Jairam suggests to the man's wife, ignoring the growing look of anxiety in my face. 'He's from Boston, visiting.'

I make another protesting motion, but Mrs Sengupta is studying my face as if it were a map.

'He's been begging them for days to let him die. But there are laws against it,' she says. 'They're worried that they will be arrested for killing him.'

From the corner of my eye I see the blanket move. Madhav Sengupta is suddenly alert. He is about seventy years old, small and neatly appointed, with a trim white beard. There's a surprisingly youthful note in his voice. I recognize the rounded lilt of Bengali – my mother tongue – in his English.

'They've been trying morphine for days, but it doesn't seem to move the pain,' he says.

Indeed, there's a plastic bag of morphine hanging by the bedside, but dripping medicine into his veins at a comically sluggish rate that would hardly touch a toothache.

'Well, perhaps they can give more morphine,' I suggest.

'But what if even the bigger dose doesn't keep away the pain?' he asks.

'Then they can give even more.'

'And then? What if I ask for more?'

He knows that I know the answer. Eventually, the morphine will carry him beyond the hollow valley of his consciousness.

There is a long pause, while he considers the next step. I sense a missile-like mind under the blanket, a restless and seeking mind, coiled like a confined spring.

'Is there any method for them to measure my pain? Like a blood test, or a cardiogram?' he asks. 'Is there an instrument to measure it?'

I shake my head: 'No. There's no such instrument. You are the measure.'

Both of us know where this line of questioning is leading. It is a kabuki dance that two must dance together. And so I continue, speaking carefully now: 'But if there's even the slightest hint of your words slurring, or of your mind slowing, or even the barest sign of delirium, they'll have to stop the morphine.'

Madhav Sengupta looks at me with the studied lightness of a man who knows that something enormous has passed between us. Mrs

Sengupta interrupts. Would I like some tea? She pours out cups of a dark, sweet liquid from a Thermos. We talk about the unseasonable weather, and the rising cost of vegetables in Delhi. As I leave the room, Mr Sengupta stirs again.

'Thank you,' he says, barely audibly, and wraps his face back in the blanket.

The next morning, I am awakened at eight o'clock by a phone call. It's Mr Sengupta's son-in-law. There are no pleasantries to begin the conversation.

'Did you recommend that they euthanize my father-in-law?' he asks. The sentence is flung across the phone line with such precise and potent fury that, were it a bolt of electricity, it would electrocute my right ear.

'Of course not,' I stammer. This, in fact, is absolutely truthful: the word 'euthanasia' was not uttered once during our conversation.

'He has been asking to increase the dose of morphine every hour, complaining of pain. The doctors insist that it's not safe. But every time they send someone to examine him, he is perfectly lucid. He just keeps telling them that he needs additional doses to keep the pain away.'

The trajectory of his plan is now clear to me. 'Well, if he wants pain medicines, then he wants pain medicines,' I say, as neutrally as possible. 'After all, shouldn't he be the judge of what hurts and how much?'

The son-in-law senses the impasse and rings off, thanking me, with a starched formality, for my 'help'.

'I don't know how he did it,' Jairam tells me when I return to the hospital a week later. 'It was as if he had stumbled on the magic formula. Dose by dose, they raised the morphine. He was fully conscious through it all. He laughed and joked with the nurses, and then, as if he had willed it, his breathing slowed down, and his skin grew cold, and he stopped blinking. Mrs Sengupta and I counted the breaths: sixteen a minute, fourteen, twelve and then four. Then the light went out of his eyes, and he was gone.'

I marvel at the description. It must have taken a supreme, calculated effort. I had once heard a doctor from the Netherlands give a lecture about how difficult it is to achieve such an end. The phrase the doctor had used was not 'euthanasia' but 'lucid death' – a compassionate but deliberate ending, assisted by medical experts, for a patient in terminal agony. 'The point of lucid death,' he said, 'is to retain the consciousness of dying, while blunting the agony of it. We have a whole team of experts dedicated to making such a death possible: social workers, nurses, pharmacologists, psychiatrists and palliative care doctors. But even with all the help we get, it's virtually impossible. It's more of an idea, really – not something achievable, but something desirable.'

Yet Madhav Sengupta had pulled it off by himself.

We think of death as a state, but of course it is a process. It is dying – not death – that is our primary experience; here, too, it is the labour, not its consummation, that defines the journey. As I walk out of the hospital that morning, crossing the intersection on Ring Road, I think of the astonishing deftness with which Madhav Sengupta had grasped all of this, about how much of the universe he had deciphered, with such clarity, under his blanket. ∎

AUTHOR'S NOTE: *I have changed the names, dates, location and many identifying details of the patients to preserve their anonymity. The conversations are paraphrased from my recollection.*

GRANTA

UNDERLAND

Robert Macfarlane

I could not have known, when we entered the underland, that it would have its own stone saint – stood in her niche in the rift's curved roof, hundreds of feet into the earth. I only saw her as we returned, though she must have watched us pass on the inward journey, pushing deeper down the fissure with the stream cold at our shins, on towards the cascades, the dry silence of the lower chamber and the undivable sump.

Her niche was of bright white dripstone, but she was picked out in mica that glittered blackly in my torch beam. Her arms were folded, her elbows sharply out, her garment flared, and her head was turned in profile to the left. There was something of the flamenco dancer to her, and something Marian also. She was nothing more or less remarkable than a speleothem – a mineral deposit chance-formed over thousands of years by chemical action in the limestone of the rift. But her presence there made sense to me: geology as theology, working to sculpt an elaborate effigy for that baroque space.

I grew up close to karst country, in rural north Nottinghamshire: twenty miles or so east of the carboniferous limestone of Derbyshire's White Peak region. The Peak was the nearest high ground to us, and so that was where we often day-tripped as a family: into the steep-sided valleys that had once been river tunnels of vast gauge, their broad ceilings long since collapsed, hopping across the polished stepping stones at Dovedale, and following field tracks past stunted trees, stunned sheep and hunkered-down hill farms. Once we visited the fluorite show-caverns at Castleton, and returned from the gift shop with polished pie wedges of rare Blue John. Sometimes we met cavers, gophering up from holes in the ground or trooping along paths in boiler-suited lines.

'All this country is hollow,' wrote Arthur Conan Doyle of the White Peak. 'Could you strike it with some gigantic hammer it would boom like a drum, or possibly cave in altogether and expose some huge subterranean sea.' He might have written the same of any karst landscape, for the first fact of limestone is its solubility in rainwater. Rain absorbs carbon dioxide from the air as it falls, creating a solution of carbonic acid that is sharp enough to fret limestone, given time. This fretting causes limestone's surface perforations of swale, gryke and clint, and also its internal labyrinths of rakes, veins, rifts and chambers. Streams wear patiently away at hillsides until they have bored out systems of astonishing topological complexity. Far below ground, starless rivers pool in caverns big enough to hold churches.

Yes, karst country is cave country, and if you spend enough time on limestone, you begin to understand how it is structured by absence as much as presence. You start to intuit the networks of pure volume that spread beneath field, moor, street, cemetery, factory and woodland, hollowed from the rock by the patient action of water. You learn to notice the portals that give access to this underland – the mine mouths, spring sites, gills and pots; the point where a stream vanishes into its own bed; the boulder-choke on a hillside that opens onto the ceiling of some immense chamber.

Limestone is globally ubiquitous. It makes up around a tenth of the volume of all sedimentary rocks. It is possible, therefore, to conceive of an archipelago of karst landscapes spread across the world, such that the Julian Alps of Slovenia, the sinkhole regions of Florida, the Israel–Palestine anticline, the Yucatan Peninsula of Mexico, the Appalachian highlands, the subterranean bat roosts of Borneo, the gorge lands of the Ardèche and the Pyrenees, the Irish Aran Islands, Wulong County in China and the Yorkshire Dales of England all exist in a familial relationship: all riddled by cave and water, all possessing complex and scarcely mapped underlands.

Of that karstic family is the White Peak, and of the White Peak's underland is Giant's Hole, an extensive and convoluted system of passages, chambers and watercourses, the entry to which lies just off the Sparrowpit Road between Chapel-en-le-Frith and Castleton, and it was into the labyrinth of Giant's Hole that I descended with three friends on a bright autumn morning.

There were several good reasons not to go underground that day. First: we would be following a stream down into the earth, and the weather forecast was for the 'second child of Tropical Storm Nadine' to hit the area that evening, bringing flooding. I did not want to be in a rift when the water level started rising. Second: Giant's has the highest concentration of radon ever measured in a limestone cave. Third: far into the system there was a squeeze feature called the 'Vice' to negotiate, the description of which made me glad I'd already had my children. Fourth: the previous night I had made the mistake of reading the cave-rescue reports for the area, and discovered that a man had died in Giant's only a year earlier, killed by exhaustion and hypothermia as he tried to return. And fifth – surely the best reason of all – was that the surface was looking so very beautiful: bright white sunshine, frost in the dips of the fields, the earth steaming where the sun caught it, red apples on green trees, a glowing daytime moon, and crows carrying silver on their wings. Who would wish to leave such a world behind?

But there it was: we were going down Giant's, so we sorted and laid out the gear on the grass in John's back garden: elektron caving ladders, karabiners, helmets with head-torches, thirty metres of nine-millimetre rope, slings for the abseils. There were four of us. John, an old friend and formidable adventurer, who had led expeditions in Antarctica and the Himalayas, and in whose company I usually felt close to invulnerable. John's son Robin, slender and tall, a folk musician and a fearless rock climber, and 'happy as a rat in a drainpipe' when below ground, according to John. Robin's cheery friend Lorna, to whom the prospect of the descent appeared no more intimidating than a trip to the supermarket. And me: fascinated by the subterranean realm, but unsure of my ability to withstand its pressures.

As we drove up to Castleton, John reminisced about some of his previous caving exploits. For years, he said, his caving partner had been a dwarf known to his friends as Dennis the Midget. Dennis was legendary for his ability to get through spaces that most people couldn't, but he had nevertheless once got stuck in a tight feature in Oxlow Cavern, not far from Giant's. John had already wriggled through the squeeze; the other member of the group, Steve, was waiting behind Dennis. 'But Dennis got well wedged, and so we had to *saw* him out,' John recalled nostalgically. 'I had him by his wrists, Steve had him by his ankles, and by pulling backwards and forwards we eventually worked him free.'

We turned off the Sparrowpit Road, thumped down a potholed farm track and parked up. John put on his caving clothes: an olive-green fleece-lined onesie, over which went a set of well-used waterproofs. I eked and grunted into my wetsuit, performing the contortionist's dance necessary to get an oversized man into undersized neoprene. We tested our lamps, rigged the rope, coiled the caving ladders and John packed a battered WWII ammunition box with what he referred to as a 'safety kit' (two candles, a lighter, two chocolate bars, five sticking plasters).

A caver with a pointy beard and dirty legs wandered up to us. He had just come out of Giant's.

'Where're you heading?'

'Garland's Pot, the Crabwalk, down the Cascades to the Eating House,' said John. 'Then maybe through the sump and back via the roof. How's the water down there?'

'Not too bad. It was chunky a couple of weeks ago, but it's thinned out a bit now.'

John looked glad. I felt sick.

The entrance to Giant's is a head-height hole in a half-cliff of crumbling limestone, set into a grassy shoulder of field. The stone where it shows is silver-grey. The cave mouth is black. Sheep grazed the upper world, and we followed a chuckling stream through the portal and into the darkness.

Why go low? It is a counter-intuitive action, running against the grain of sense and the gradient of the spirit. You descend far from day. The mountaineer Joe Simpson has written of the 'inverted gravity' that draws people up towards the summits of peaks, often at the risk of their own lives; a rarer force pulls people down into what Cormac McCarthy – in his great karst novel, *Child of God* – calls 'the awful darkness inside the world'. Culture is rife with warnings against travel into the depths, from Orpheus through Dante to H.G. Wells. Psychopomps are almost always needed: specialist guides (Horus, Hecate, Virgil, Odin, Mercury) who can foresee danger and navigate the forking blackness. The experience of being underground is what psychologists call 'aversive'. Claustrophobia intimidates the mind and twitches the muscles; accounts of confined spaces can clutch at the heart of a person standing safely in clear air. The mind's reaction to confined spaces feels hard-wired, and caving requires almost as its first skill the ability to dismantle one's instinctive neural alarm systems.

For these reasons, the underland is a stranger, less frequented region than the realm of mountains. Relatively few people know of it, fewer still have the wish or the means to enter it voluntarily. Yet of those who do, many find themselves gripped by obsession. They develop tunnel vision. Cavers are driven in particular by a desire to uncover new passages and chambers, and to connect apparently separate systems. Within caving communities, rumours circulate about entry points that might give access to previously unwitnessed spaces. Secrets are closely guarded, jealously shared.

Passions run high in part because the yields can be extraordinary. Because it is resistant to the vision of the satellitic eye that scans and maps the surface world, we know relatively little about the underland, and remarkable finds remain possible. In the Mendips in south-west England, a side tunnel was painstakingly dug free of silt and boulders – four hours' digging every Tuesday night for four years – until in 2012 the team at last broke into a cavern whose walls sparkled with white calcite flowstone: they named it the Frozen Deep. The Mendips breakthrough was a sideshow compared to the discovery on New Year's Day 1999 of Titan, a natural cavern within a few miles of Giant's Hole that includes the deepest shaft known in Britain (almost five hundred feet deep, and segmented at a height of two hundred feet from its base by a wide frill of rock now known as the Event Horizon). It is inconceivable that any new mountain might now be found in the British Isles – but the deepest cave to date lay unfound until the last year of the twentieth century. The deepest cave, and the oldest art also: in 2011, an archaeologist exploring a limestone cave on the Gower Peninsula in South Wales happened upon what is arguably the most ancient petroglyph in northern Europe – a flint engraving of a speared reindeer, dated to 14,000 years ago, incised when most of what is now Wales was under a mantle of glaciers.

The underland is also a wonderland: it is down a rabbit hole that Alice falls on her voyage of marvels and curiosity, a dream-shaft that leads to a topsy-turvy place. Two days' travel into the Llangattock system of North Wales, a team of cavers last year found a human-sized helictite-encrusted stalactite of pale flowstone, which they christened the Courtesan. In 2007, a thousand feet below the Chihuahuan Desert in Mexico, two brothers following a lead seam in a mine drilled their way into a cavern that was criss-crossed by hundreds of calcium sulphite crystals: translucent blades of mineral up to forty feet long, which jagged through the cave's interior like toppled obelisks.

Encouraged by the possibility of such discoveries, different groups of underland explorers perfect different methods of investigation. As well as diggers, there are detonators, dyers, divers and dowsers. In the karst of Tennessee – rich with cave art, extensive beyond knowledge – men drive around with sticks of explosive in the back of their trucks searching for new entrances, ready to bomb their way in. In the Pyrenees, fluorescin is poured into streams where they enter the earth, staining them brilliant green, so that their rates of underground flow can be measured and their debouchements mapped. At Wookey Hole in Somerset, cave-diving was developed during the 1940s as an exploratory technique, using home-made respirators to plumb the depths of what slowly revealed itself as a huge flooded system. While up on the surface, cars hurtled along the A39 and the bells of Wells Cathedral sounded the hours, down below diver after diver drowned in the underwater tunnels, failed by jerry-built equipment or lost in the labyrinth.

In Slovenia, cavers walk the hillsides carrying feathers tucked into their packs, so that they can test for slight breezes coming out of cracks or stone piles, which might indicate the existence of a new portal (pneumatics as navigation). In South Wales between 1955 and 1995 a man called Peter Harvey, a pioneer of British cave exploration, devoted his life to the exploration of Ogof Ffynnon Ddu – the Cave of the Black Spring – a system which is now known to stretch for more than forty miles. Harvey's caving diaries and photographs record four decades and around nine hundred trips into Black Spring, including the repeated diving of flooded sumps. He also walked hundreds of miles above ground with hazel sticks in hand – hoping in this way to dowse out the routes of the underground watercourses he could not see.

That day in Giant's, I began to understand how such subterranean obsessions might be inspired, for the hours we spent down there were among the strangest and most memorable I have known at any altitude. From the cave's mouth came a hundred yards of narrowing, twisting tunnel, the stream sounding louder as the space closed in. After the first curve the cave mouth was invisible; after the fourth so was daylight.

John led and we splashed after him in single file. The surface of the rock that enfolded us was in places smooth as baize to the eye but raspy to the touch. Elsewhere it was adorned with glistening dimples and tentacles of stone, or weirdly fungal nets. We tend to think of erosion only as a process of subtraction, but in limestone what is dissolved by water is often re-precipitated elsewhere, resulting in accretion and slow growth. This is the origin of stalagmites and stalactites, but also of the ornate drapery and slow-motion tumbles of dripstone. There are no straight lines or clean angles in karst. Curve, crease, pleat and whorl are the units of its topology; perpendiculars, rectilinears and points its anathema; the fold its principal form. In all these respects it is a pure geology of the baroque.

We entered a high chamber, down one face of which ran a dripstone cascade perhaps fifteen feet high, all bosses and drips and gelid rapids, shining beneath its lacquer of water and criss-crossed by sparkling veins of biotite. It had the appearance of an altar, magnificent in its wrought and tearful flow, devoted to the iteration of embellishment. When I looked up, I could see no roof to the chamber but only further darkness, out of which arced falling drops of water to gleam in my head-torch beam.

Beyond the altar, back in the rift, the noise began to increase.

'Slowly now,' John said. 'We're getting near Garland's.'

The sound rose to a roar. Abruptly, the floor of the tunnel ended. John stood with a guard-arm out as I approached the edge. Garland's was a rough cylinder of space, perhaps twelve feet in diameter and twenty feet deep, and the stream thundered over its rim and into the belly of the pot. Lorna and I sat on pillows of karst while John and Robin leaned out over the pot to set up a ladder and safety rope from a pair of in situ bolts.

One by one, with John belaying us on the safety rope from above, we dangled down the thin wire ladder. Unused to the technique, I swung across into the path of the cascade, which pummelled me on the head and back.

John swarmed down last. 'Once, I got back to this point to find that some fucker had stolen my ladder,' he said. 'I had to climb out from here unroped. I was very annoyed.'

I looked back up at the slick vertical rock. It was impossible to imagine making that climb. I hoped no fucker stole our ladder.

The base walls of the pot were sheer and solid, except for a narrow cleft which showed as a rift of blackness, and into which the stream led. John approached the cleft and turned sideways. 'Welcome to the

Crabwalk,' he said, and disappeared into it shoulder first. I followed, clanking the ammo box against the walls, filling the rift with noise.

I was in the Crabwalk for perhaps three hours, including the retreat. It is a space so extraordinary that common language serves barely even to sketch it. It is between sixty and a hundred feet high, and between three feet and eight inches wide. Its sides billow out and dip in. It twists and turns. No – those verbs fall hopelessly short of its tortuousness. It chicanes, it hairpins, it ogees, it sines, it spindles, it intestines, it volutes. No one could enter it and preserve their sense of orientation. If you somehow filled it with concrete and then cut away the land that surrounds it, you would be left with a vast umbilicus or flattened unicorn's horn, dipping and coiling its way lower and lower. Each new curve emerges from its predecessor rather as pleat might be shaken from pleat in the unfurling of a cloth, or turn is born always from turn in the course of a stream.

Navigating the Crabwalk has aspects both of the rebus and the assault course. Despite its name, it is not something along which you walk. I dipped, squashed, curved, 'udged' (a caver's verb) and poured myself down it, always leading with a shoulder, clothes rasping against the limestone, feet in the rushing stream, head clashing off knoll and billow, body flattened and scaped by the stone's own forms. I had expected language to be diminished by the data-depleted darkness of the underland and its curtailed cognitive spaces, but instead, it flowed and flowered, and I wanted new words for this new world, a liquid language for a liquid landscape, and sounds and syllables began to meld into one another, forming ruchey new cocklings and portmanteau meltings – rift-riffs and speleotropes – or folding out of and back onto one another (re-plying, multi-plying), for the rift was a Möbius strip gone mad, and travelling it was like pushing through the voluptuous interior of a theatre curtain. It was a headlong whole-body part-plummet that I did not want to end but then the Vice stopped us dead.

I was close behind John when he halted. Ahead, the left-hand side of the rift bulged out at belly level, the right-hand side was its matching convex and the gutter of the rift had been cut sharply away beneath the bulge, leaving little foothold. The curved gap between the sides was perhaps nine inches across at its tightest. Where we had stopped, the rift was so narrow that we could not turn our heads. So we stood there together, bodies side-on to the left wall, arms up as if at gunpoint, palms flat on the stone, heads locked sideways, breathing hard. I had the dissonant sense of vertical space opening vastly above me, and extreme lateral confinement. I could see the back of John's skull. John could see the problem ahead. Somewhere behind us were Lorna and Robin, taking their time.

'This looks seriously tight, Rob. Wait here.'

John udged on. I could see more of the problem now; could see his feet tickling vainly for purchase on the undercut. The trick was to use upper-body strength to lift yourself above the pinch-point, and then shift forwards before dropping down again where the rift re-widened. But John had had shoulder surgery two months earlier, and was obviously finding it hard to hoist himself up and on.

He udged back. 'I don't like it. I don't trust my shoulder to get me through, and if I slip, I might wedge.'

'Then you'll have to starve yourself free,' I said. 'That could take some time.'

No reply. I waited. He had another go, and this time vanished from view. Sounds of foot-scuffling and nylon scraping on rock. Grunts. An anxious shout, then a yell.

'I'm through.'

I followed him. The problem was – that wasn't the Vice. We found the Vice a few folds further on, and its form was diabolical: an even tighter gap, even more risk of wedging. There seemed to be just enough room to wriggle through sideways beneath the pinch-point, but that would involve crouching down in the stream and I did not cherish the thought of getting stuck so close to water level.

John wasn't eager to proceed. 'Sorry, Rob. I'm having a moment. It's my shoulder. I'm worried about getting stuck.'

I offered to try it. We reversed the first squeeze, back to where there was more room, and I clambered up and over John. I was about to proceed when I glanced down at the stream. The water, previously clear as glass, had turned a silty brown.

'John, the water's muddying,' I said. 'Does that mean rain on the surface?'

'Probably. A bit. Don't worry – there's no storm big enough to flood this rift: it's over sixty feet deep. We'd just climb the walls, or float up between them.'

I disliked either outcome. John seemed unworried.

It took me a minute or so to crack the knack of the Vice. You needed to hook a little under-ledge with your toes, hope they didn't slip, breathe out to empty your lungs and flatten your chest, then slip through and gasp for air on the other side. I hooked, exhaled, flattened, slipped, gasped.

'Are you past it?'

I was, and it felt as if I had stepped through a heavy door which had then slammed shut behind me. Ahead was the empty rift and behind, on the other side of the Vice, were John, Lorna, Robin and the surface. Claustrophobia surged. It came first as a prickling in the scalp, and then a tightness in the lungs. My heart rate leaped and my whole skin felt as if it were being pressed inwards, crumpled down to a dark central point. Images of the open crowded my mind: two swans flying upwind at head height, beating away on wide white wings; a three-quarters moon three-quarters of the way up the sky; flickering grass.

There are many ways to die underground. There is death by drowning, death by crushing, death by exhaustion, death by falling, death by starvation, death by cold. Certainly the most infamous death in British caving history is the Neil Moss tragedy. It is still – in my experience – a story people in Derbyshire do not like to discuss, half a century on.

Moss was a philosophy student from Balliol College, Oxford, and an experienced caver. In mid-March 1959, after the end of the academic term, he travelled to the White Peak, and warmed up with a successful descent of Giant's Hole. The following weekend, he decided to join a BSA (British Speleological Association) exploratory trip into the further reaches of Peak Cavern, near Castleton. Beyond the Peak's well-known 'Great Chamber' – a show-cave since the nineteenth century – were a series of obstacles, which had already been forced by earlier BSA groups: a long semi-siphon known as the Mucky Ducks, a boulder passage which had to be traversed at full length, an awkward bend with a muddy sump, and then – at the top of a mud slope – a narrow eyehole in the limestone, through which it is just possible to wriggle a human body. After the eyehole came a small thigh-deep lake. Beyond that was the unknown.

The group entered Peak Cavern on the Sunday, reached and crossed the lake, and at that point Moss volunteered to take the lead. He arrived into a small cave, from the floor of which descended a narrow fissure. This fissure was the focus of the group's exploration.

Moss was a tall, slim young man. He decided to lower an elektron ladder into the pot and see how far he could get. The pot was vertical for thirty-five feet, and then curved round and across with a corkscrew twist, before making a sharp elbow bend back to the vertical. With some difficulty, Moss negotiated the elbow bend, only to discover that the pot then became choked with boulders. He could feel the boulders with his feet, but the pot was so narrow that he couldn't use his hands to move them. The fissure had – in the language of caving – deaded out. He began to re-ascend the pot. A few yards below the elbow he slipped a little, lost his grip on the ladder and became stuck.

Moss could not bend his legs to gain purchase on the rungs of the ladder with his feet, which were anyway slippery with clay. He could not move his arms to clasp the ladder again with his fingers. Every movement he made to re-grip the ladder caused him to slide a little further down the fissure, become a little more wedged. The limestone soon had him fast.

So began one of the largest cave-rescue attempts mounted in Britain at that date. The rescuers themselves took extreme risks in their attempts to save Moss. Ropes were repeatedly lowered to him, but he could not hold them. Soda lime was carried in to absorb the build-up of carbon dioxide. Heavy oxygen cylinders were wrestled through the Mucky Ducks and pushed by head and hand along the boulder passage. Hundreds of metres of telephone line were threaded through the system to link the fissure to the surface. Two young men hauled a twelve-volt car battery through the passages to provide energy for light.

But Moss still died, over the course of two days, gradually stifled as the oxygen content in the shaft decreased and the carbon dioxide content built up. When his death was confirmed, his father – who had rushed to Castleton and was staying in a local hotel, waiting for news from within the caves – decided that no one else was to hazard their lives trying to retrieve his son's body. It had begun to rain heavily, and the rescuers were at risk of drowning as the water levels rose. Concrete was later poured down the fissure, entombing Moss's corpse. The chamber beneath which he had died was named in his memory.

An old caving joke: 'How do you kill yourself if you get stuck caving? Bite your own tongue off and then swallow it so it gets stuck in your throat and you asphyxiate!' Laugh? I nearly choked.

We held a shouted conference at the Vice. John didn't want to risk it. I was keen to press further on into the system. Robin was happy to join me. So John and Lorna would return to Garland's and wait for us there. It was impossible to get lost as there was only one route down the rift. We agreed a turnaround time, and the hour at which John should assume a problem had occurred, and seek help.

Robin snaked through the Vice, and we went on together. I was glad to have company again. We moved fast, swapping leads, handing the ammo box from person to person as we met obstacles, squeezes or drops. Below the Vice, the rift steepened its slope, and we soon encountered the first of the cascades, where the stream dropped eight feet off a smooth lip into a deep plunge pool. Two sharp fins of rock extended over the drop, and we used them to lean out before hanging down to find footing on the plunge pool's sides. The second cascade was bigger, ten feet or so, and had a rusting iron ladder in place, which lay loose against the rock. We clambered down it, the stream bashing our shoulders as we went, the ladder screeching as it dragged across the karst.

Once, when Robin was ahead and the rift widened, I turned off my light and sat on a bench of dripstone for a few minutes. The darkness that I entered there was without feature, a darkness impossible above ground, a darkness so total that it was only disrupted by the firework flashes and red retinal squiggles that came when I closed my eyes.

We were running short of time when the stream suddenly dropped away through a hole in the rift's floor, into some unplumbable further fold of the labyrinth. We followed the bed of the stream's former course, and after a few minutes the gradient eased, and we turned a corner to find ourselves in a wide dry chamber. To right and left, it had raised and flattened areas, like the upper bunks in a dormitory. Through its centre the stream had cut a narrow gorge ten or twelve feet deep. We clambered up to the right-hand dormitory and stopped briefly there, listening to the silence. I could hear my own heartbeat.

This, I guessed, was the Eating House. It was a lonely, deep place, and beyond it were lonelier and deeper places still – Geological Pot, an eighty-foot pot that dwarfed Garland's, and had to be rappelled down; the desperate crossing to Oxlow Cavern; the sump along which, if it were dry enough, we would have to crawl on our backs, noses and mouths pressed against the roof of the shallow tunnel, breathing the available air there, after which would come the roped traverse back along the roof of the Crabwalk. To any competent caver, these were possible adventures. To me, without John's guidance, they were territories as remote and unreachable as the moon.

So Robin and I turned round and began the climb back out, retracing the rift's route. It was just above the upper cascade, or perhaps it was just below it, that I glanced up and saw there, in the pool of my head-torch beam, the black-mica figure standing clear in her pale dripstone niche. I called to Robin, and he came back, and we studied her for a minute or so, trying to understand something of her origin and her significance.

Then it was on back up through the rift, a squeeze and a slither past the Vice, and at last we stepped out of the confines of the Crabwalk and into the openness of Garland's Pot. There were John and Lorna waiting for us, there was the stream deepening the pot millimetre by millimetre, and there was our ladder, unstolen – so we swayed back up it one by one and swung across onto the slippery ledges at the pot's top. Back past the dripstone altar, back up the widening tunnel, and we smelled the surface before we saw it: gusts of clean air, green and strange in the nose, and then a rough door of sunshine ahead. Yellow light. Dilated pupils. A crow's caw.

We stood in the cave mouth, took off our helmets, grinned.

'It's nice to be back in a world of colour,' said Lorna.

'I'd forgotten that sheep existed,' I said.

Later, John drove me up a sidetrack to the upper edge of a vast flux quarry. He'd seen peregrines there a couple of times recently, and wanted to check on them. Cumulonimbus boiled overhead, folding out of themselves in impossible performances of volume. Ravens tumbled and curved on the updraughts. The quarry's cliffs were two hundred feet high in places. The lake of water on its floor was coppery blue-green. A car had been run off the edge at some point, and now lay rusting and smashed in the lake. We scrambled over tiles of asbestos to the quarry rim, and startled a big dog fox which flowed away from us, orange over the boulders, then poured himself into a cleft in the quarry wall. We waited to see if he would emerge again. It was late afternoon, and the light on the eastern hills was low and slant-wise, throwing into relief the cloughs and stream-cuts of the moor, glinting on the gritstone outcrops and the limestone rakes, showing up the hollowness of the land, such that the whole visible world seemed like something to be walked not over but into. ∎

Eternities

A child lifted in his mother's arms to see a parade
And that old man throwing breadcrumbs
To the pigeons crowding around his feet in the park,
Could they be the same person?

The blind woman who may know the answer recalls
Seeing a ship as big as a city block
Glide one night all lit up past her kitchen window
On its way to the dark and stormy Atlantic.

NUESTRA SEÑORA DE LA ASUNCIÓN

Lina Wolff

TRANSLATED FROM THE SWEDISH BY SASKIA VOGEL

Once I met a writer who said he couldn't bear to be a writer any more. It was at a party in Madrid and I don't remember how I ended up there, but it was on Calle de Ventura de la Vega so I assume it was someone I met that night who had taken me there (my own friends, to the extent that I even had any, lived in completely different places). If you really are a writer you can't stop just like that, I said. I have to, he said then. Because I feel I'm gravitating towards madness, and the days I'm not gravitating towards madness, I gravitate towards something even worse. What? I said. He said he didn't know, but he had his wife and child to think of and that as far as madness went he believed, like Roberto Bolaño, that it was contagious.

During this time I didn't go out often. I was newly married and spoke Spanish badly. My son was about a year old and I was always home – except every now and again when my husband returned from his travels, put his bags down in the hall and looked at me, sitting on the sofa after days glued to the soap operas. I used to toss the caramel wrappers right on the floor and when I drained the soda cans I placed them in the bookshelf behind the sofa. The chewed-up gum went in the flowerpot on the floor. I must have looked bloated and envious sitting there on the sofa when my husband came home. He always wore a tie and a glossy suit and when he stood there with his coal-black Spanish hair it was as if you could see the world's airports in his eyes. But he never commented on the mess or that I looked like someone who hadn't washed their hair in a week. He said: Now it's your turn to go out. And he picked up our son who started to scream. Our son vomited big yellow smears on his suit but he just laughed and looked happy. Spaniards love children.

They are both well dressed and laid-back; I have always liked the combination.

Because I was out so seldom I sometimes thought I'd forgotten how to talk to people. That the writer who didn't want to be a writer was the first person at the party I exchanged a few words with was to be expected, I thought – I sit at home for weeks, maybe months – and when I finally get out and talk to someone it's with a writer who thinks he's going mad. After the madness thing, he said, he had the urge for completely unbridled sex. *Tengo ganas de sexo desenfrenado*, he said. *Estoy mas salida que el pico de una mesa*, he said as well and exactly what that meant I didn't understand at the time. Where are you from? he asked later and then I said that I came from France. Why did I say that? Possibly because people in Latin countries don't really take you seriously when you say you're from Sweden. Or so that he, in his current frame of mind, wouldn't confuse me with some topless swimmer from 1980s Benidorm.

I continued to mingle. The next person I spoke with was a woman who introduced herself as Filomena. This is a party for people who have problems, she said. No one here is normal except you, and you're not even from Spain. I asked what she did, and she said that her husband owned a bar. I told her about the writer I had just talked to and she said she knew him, at this party almost everyone knew each other, and tomorrow they were taking a coach to Granada and this was just a pre-party, or not a pre-party but a kind of run-up. Coach all the way to Granada? I said and she nodded. Do you have a mobile number? she asked later.

It was four in the morning when I got home to the apartment on Calle Embajadores. My husband was asleep with the child in our bed and I went to sleep on the sofa in the living room so I wouldn't wake them. It was a warm, dark night. An unnatural night, as nights in Madrid are because Madrid is an unnatural city, situated where no city should be, without natural greenery and water. I remembered something the writer had said, that the most frightening thing about madness is that there isn't an obvious border between being healthy and being sick. That's just how it is, he said, things that seem strange suddenly feel completely normal. I felt quite well because right then I couldn't think of anything that felt normal; on the contrary, everything in my life seemed very strange and kind of pursed and illogical. I wished I'd said that to the writer. Maybe he would have said I was fine. But on the other hand – if a crazy person tells you you're fine, what does that mean? In my half-drunkenness I couldn't figure it out.

At seven o'clock, Filomena called my mobile. The sun had started to climb and the sky over Madrid was light blue with white airplane trails. From the window I could see a few dog owners with their dogs in the park. They spoke in small groups while the dogs ran around and peed, even in the sandboxes where children, probably my son too, would play in a few hours. Someone dropped out, Filomena said. You can come with us to Granada. It may not be a luxurious trip, it's organized by the Madrid local authority, but you, being from France, might get a kick out of getting out and seeing a new place. I said I didn't know. My husband got home yesterday. But this is still a great opportunity, she said then. I woke my husband up and asked him what he thought and he said of course you should go, one has to see Granada. I packed a little bag, showered quickly and went down to the street. Grabbed a coffee at a bar and then the subway to Méndez Álvaro where the coach would be waiting. Everyone from the party stood there, just out of the shower and ready to start the day and the journey. I said hello. The writer was there too and today he didn't look a bit mad. *Tu vas bien?* he said and I answered, *Mais oui.* Then we packed into the coach and I felt there was something industrial in the way they handled us. The coach was old and brown. This feels kind of like an Almodóvar film, I said. The writer and Filomena looked at me blankly.

The engine started and the coach began to move. We drove out of Madrid and there was almost no traffic at all. You could sit and look at the houses in peace. Sometimes I did that when we drove around in our car. I would sit and look at the houses we drove past, feeling something at the bottom of my stomach, a kind of great terror I was always trying to hold back. When you drove on the circular you could sometimes see right into people's dining rooms. You could see them sitting around tables and eating some ten, twenty metres away.

'The most fascinating thing about Madrid,' I said to the writer, who was sitting next to me, 'is the coexistence of so many dimensions. Everything is wall to wall: motorways, living rooms, people from South America and people from Europe. We all live with only a few metres or sometimes only decimetres between us. I, for example, have no idea who sleeps on the other side of my bedroom wall.'

'It's true,' answered the writer. 'Everything is curiously put together here. Maybe it feels exotic to someone like you, who comes from elsewhere. But all of this coexistence means that nothing has a real identity, least of all the city itself.'

We sat in silence for a while. Around Aranjuez, Filomena leaned forward and whispered in my ear that she and the writer had made love after I left the party.

'Did you?' I said.

'Yes,' said Filomena. 'And he might look harmless, but in bed he becomes . . . He forces you to do all sorts of things.'

She shook her hand in front of her as if she had burned herself. I laughed at her.

'So, was it good, though?' I said.

'Good if you are like me,' she answered then, 'because I can be both predator and prey at the same time.'

Suddenly, I didn't feel like laughing any more. I blushed without knowing why. The writer stared intently out the window.

There were actually far too many of us in the coach. I didn't have high expectations, but a little space to put away my bag, stretch my legs and rest my hands in my lap without poking somebody in the side with my elbow was, I felt, the least one could ask for, even if I had been given a free ride. But the coach was crowded, and I couldn't help feeling I was bothering the writer every time I moved, like when

I changed the batteries in the camera or when I started to eat the tuna baguette that I'd bought in the subway. Filomena sat silently behind us, her legs crossed. She ran her hand through her hair now and again and I thought she might be upset because I was the one sitting with the writer, not her. I suggested that he change seats, which they both agreed to immediately. The writer sat behind me with Filomena and I now had two seats to myself. Across the aisle sat a man who was travelling alone. I looked at him and he looked right back at me. He had the curious, pale gaze of the demented. A gaze that seems to see things no one else sees. He smiled at me, and it was an honest and open smile. I smiled back for a while. Then I couldn't keep it up any more and turned away and looked out the window again.

'What's your diagnosis?' I heard Filomena ask behind me.

'You know very well that there are certain unwritten rules on trips like these,' the writer answered. 'You don't talk to each other much, and if you do talk, you never talk about diagnoses or illnesses.'

The brown bus continued inland, through the heat. We all sat in silence, looked out the windows at the landscape gliding by. Sometimes sand-coloured villages emerged from the earth like ghost towns. One village climbed up a ledge above a ravine; it looked like it was struggling to hold on but at any moment it could lose its grip and fall down. Now and then the guide from Madrid's local authority spoke into the microphone. He had a gently condescending tone. I soon stopped listening to what he was saying. I closed my eyes and leaned back in the seat. I sat like that for a long time. The air conditioner was on high; it was the only sound and the hum was monotonous and calming.

'At last, we are in Granada,' the guide announced a few hours later.

The coach had stopped by the Alhambra and we got out and stood in a crescent in the car park. A new, local guide arrived to take care of us. He wasn't a Spaniard either; maybe he was from Morocco. We followed him through the Arabic walkways and heard water gurgling from the atria. The hot wind stirred in the branches of the cypresses and the stone building radiated a heat that almost burned when you came close.

'Hell must feel like the Arctic Circle compared to this,' someone said.

The writer and Filomena held on to each other; they didn't seem to care that they were the only two people I knew on this trip and that I was now walking by myself. I called my husband at home in Madrid, asked how it was going and he said don't think about us, make sure to meet people and have fun. It's not *that* much fun, I said and he replied that everything is what you make of it. We went on through walkways, courtyards and rooms, and came to some sort of cafeteria where we drank Arabic tea. Our faces blazed and our tongues burned and the writer said that he didn't understand how the Arabs in their time could drink such hot tea in this heat.

'Cure ill with ill,' the guide said.

We sweated and looked at the walls, which were covered in winding patterns.

'If you're not crazy when you get here, you will be after you've sat a while and looked at these walls,' said the writer.

'The untrained eye looks in vain at Moorish art,' said the guide. 'You Westerners want to see faces and bodies everywhere.'

'Is that so?' said the writer.

'Yes, more than anything you want to see bodies,' said the guide. 'Bodies, bodies and more bodies.'

There was silence.

The guide looked at the writer and his gaze lingered as if he were very tired and had forgotten we were even there.

'You can sit there and stare as much as you like,' he said in the end. 'But the longer you look, the less you will understand.'

He got up and raised his hand in our direction as if to say we should stay. Then he was gone. We stayed behind for a while, then got up and walked to the car park.

We left Granada and the Alhambra some time in the afternoon. Once we were on the bus, the driver said the air conditioning was out of order. Filomena took out her fan and I fanned myself with a book I had in my bag. We arrived at an insignificant little church that we only stopped at because of the heat. Everyone needed to breathe and, as the guide said, there are no better places to breathe than churches. The church was called Nuestra Señora de la Asunción. We moved towards the entrance. I was last, and felt dizzy. The writer and Filomena stopped walking to let me catch up and asked how I was. I said the sweetness of the Arabic tea was still sitting high in my throat, and that I had forgotten my sunglasses in the coach.

'Take it easy, don't overdo it,' they said and went ahead of me towards the church.

It was at the entrance that I saw the mangled angel. At first I didn't understand what was wrong, and then I stopped and took a few steps back. Above the entrance to the church were five angels. They were pompous boy angels with fat hands, protruding eyes and strong jawlines, sculpted from some sort of sandstone. Four of the angels had insipid faces, but the fifth angel's features were completely distorted. I looked away. Thought: Surely that angel isn't meant to look like that. I shut my eyes, and looked again. But the fifth angel looked the same as before: it stared out over the landscape as if it had seen something terrible. Its mouth was wide open, eyes staring. The stone face emanated – in spite of the even, flat surface – a feeling of pure horror. The others in the group had gone into the church and I stood alone in the courtyard. He sees something out there, I thought, and climbed onto a bench and peered in the same direction as the angel. And there, maybe fifty metres away, I saw the black coat. It took a minute before I understood who it was. I remembered that my mother-in-law once had told me about him. She said that when you see the angel of death, you know, because he is the only one of the angels dressed all in black. Spanish superstition, I said at the time. When he looks at you, your whole body starts to sweat and you start to shake, she said seriously. Then something happens inside of you, something like a twig breaking, and nothing will be the same again. Spanish superstition, I said again and then she said that of course we in the north don't know anything about angels since they, like so much else, can't live in sub-zero temperatures.

I shut my eyes. When I opened them again I saw him clearly. He had turned towards me and stood there now, still and totally black, with the dead earth in the background. The hot wind stirred his coat and he stared at me with eyes of fire.

I must have fainted, because when I opened my eyes again I was lying inside the church and Filomena stood above me waving her fan over my face. The writer stood next to her and looked at me with anticipation, and the municipal guide stroked water on my cheeks. I remembered the angel instantly.

'I saw something out there,' I said and stood up. 'Someone standing in a black coat in the distance.'

'Ah – the priest,' said the writer, avoiding eye contact.

'Don't you start now,' the municipal guide said.

'Start what?' I asked.

'Don't play dumb,' he said. 'Just go out and sit in the coach.'

I went into the courtyard again. The pompous boy angels now looked identical. The fifth angel looked exactly like the other four – dense and even, indifferently staring ahead. I climbed onto the bench and looked out over the landscape. Black and yellow spots danced in the light, as they do in your field of vision when it gets too hot.

'I had a Sicilian lover once,' said Filomena when we were sitting in the coach again.

'Is that so?' said the writer.

'Yes, I did,' she said as if she doubted that he believed her. 'It's true.'

'I believe you,' he said.

'What are you diagnosed with?' she asked again.

And when he didn't answer:

'It's something related to anxiety, right? You can see it in your face. It looks like it's broken.'

'Don't be so hard on my face,' the writer said. 'If you'd been through what I've been through you'd be happy to have a face at all.'

Filomena snorted. We drove through a village with aluminium-framed windows and elderly people in black who sat along the walls of the houses.

When we got back to Madrid it was late. The heat from the day was stored in the asphalt and radiated from the ground when you walked on the pavement. We said our goodbyes and suddenly it felt like we were behaving politely and stiffly. Maybe we were just tired. I thought I wanted to talk to the writer about madness and normality, just comment on it quickly, hear if he also had heard the thing my mother-in-law had said about the angel of death, and what he thought the municipal guide was suggesting when he said that I shouldn't start anything. And the angel on the church – you're not necessarily crazy just because you see things in the heat, right? I thought: I'll go up to the writer and ask if he wants to go and have a drink in a bar. But the writer didn't seem to be in the mood; he stood and stroked his stubble and looked worried. Sod it, I thought. Anyway, I'm not afraid of going mad, I'm more afraid that everything will just go right to hell.

Everyone from the trip went home. I wanted to do the same but to go home like this – with a feeling of the scorched hinterland, visions and madness in general – felt wrong. I thought: To go home now would be like walking into a clean apartment with dirty shoes. So instead of taking the subway to Legazpi I took it to Goya and started to walk towards Retiro. There was a long queue outside the Renoir cinema. I joined it and bought a ticket (I asked for a ticket to any film and the woman in the window gave me one from the thickest stack in front of her). I went in and sat down in the cinema. It was painted red and had black chairs and small round lamps screwed into the walls. A few rows behind me sat two older women. They spoke hoarsely about immigrants. One said that the ones who came from the Dominican Republic were responsible for 95 per cent of the crime in her neighbourhood, and then the other asked if she had read any statistics on it and then the first one replied that you didn't need to, you understood that that's the way it was just by living there.

The film began. Sean Penn wandered around a large house on the screen. He had teased black hair and was made up like an old lady or a singer in a rock band. For the rest of the movie he pulled around a suitcase on wheels. The director, apparently Sean Penn himself, seemed to have wanted to imitate aspects of Tarantino's style, but whereas Tarantino knows what he is doing, Sean Penn didn't seem to have a clue. The ladies behind me snored loudly. I sat and thought about the trip. I thought about the writer and Filomena and wondered what exactly he had forced her to do. I tried to picture the writer forcing Filomena to do something, but it was impossible. Maybe they were lying. Maybe they had decided that they were going to tease me. And in which way was she both prey and predator? I couldn't picture that either. Then I thought about the angel of death and considered telling my husband. My husband is a rational person, but inside he has a deep Spanish vein that makes him superstitious. When you hit that vein there's no limit to what he'll believe. I also felt afraid that something would happen to our son and that the angel of death was an omen, and so I decided not to say anything to my husband because shared fear, just like shared happiness, is doubled. Then I thought about what I should eat for dinner the next night and remembered I had a can of tuna in the larder, but then I remembered that my husband was home now and that we should make sure to eat something good. That big, flat fish called dorado. Or lubina. Or just steamed black mussels from Galicia. Then I thought that it was all the same and nothing really mattered.

Out on the street again, I saw that white clouds had come in over the dark sky. They galloped fast and you felt the wind all down the streets. My mobile rang and I answered. It was Filomena.

'I saw the angel of death, too,' she said.

'What?' I said.

'I saw him, too. And so did the writer, and Juan who stayed in the bus and didn't want to go out at all.'

I remembered the pale, demented look.

'Why didn't you say?' I said.

'I am also afraid.'

'Afraid of what?'

'Suddenly everything can fall apart.'

'Exactly what can fall apart, Filomena?'

There was a rustling sound at the other end of the receiver and I thought she would hang up. But the rustling stopped and I heard her voice clearly.

'I don't know. The face, maybe. Or the face and the body. Or the face, the body and your whole life. The whole thing.'

I didn't know what to say.

'Maybe we'll talk again sometime,' I said in the end.

'I don't think so,' she said.

We hung up. When I went down into the subway I passed a man with dreadlocks, begging, a paper cup held out in front of him. I didn't put anything in it, but when I walked by I heard him whisper: *Don't give up, baby, keep on struggle, baby, everything will be fine, baby.* ■

New Fiction | from **Grove Atlantic**

August 2013

It's Not Love, It's Just Paris
Patricia Engel

"Gloriously gifted and alarmingly intelligent
. . . [Engel's] ability to pierce the hearts
of her crazy-ass characters, to fracture
a moment into its elementary particles
of yearning, cruelty, love and confusion
will leave you breathless."—Junot Díaz

GROVE PRESS

Let the Games Begin
Niccolò Ammaniti

"*Let the Games Begin* may well be
the print version of *La Dolce Vita*
set today."—*L'Unità*

BLACK CAT

August 2013

September 2013

The Woman Who Lost Her Soul
Bob Shacochis

"No one in American literature is better
at casting his imagination into the
deepest currents of American culture
and politics than Bob Shacochis. . . .
A masterpiece."
—Robert Olen Butler

ATLANTIC MONTHLY PRESS

GROVE ATLANTIC
Distributed by Publishers Group West

www.groveatlantic.com

THE MAN AT
THE RIVER

Dave Eggers

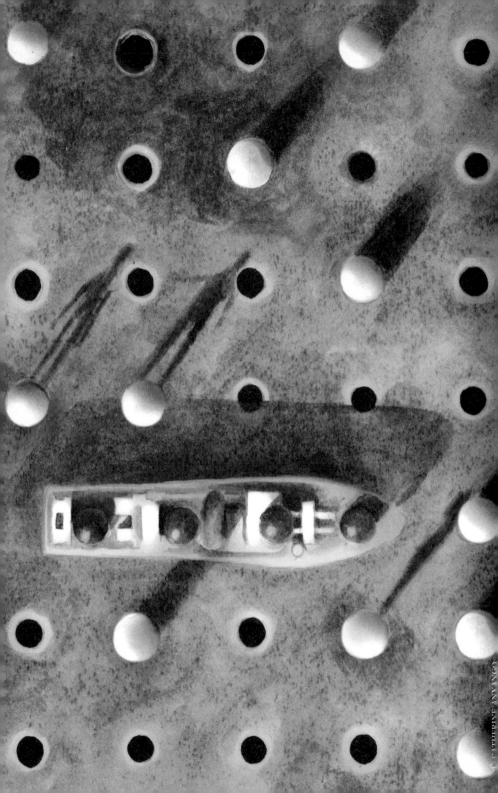

There is an American sitting by a narrow caramel-coloured river in South Sudan. His Sudanese friend, ten years his junior, has brought him to the area, and they have been touring around on bicycles, riding on dirt trails. This day, his Sudanese friend wanted to show the American man a town on the other side of the river, and so they rode a few miles to the riverbank, to this spot, where the river was shallow and slow-moving, and the Sudanese friend waded across.

But the American man decided he couldn't wade across the river. He had cut his shin a few days before, and the cut was unbandaged and deep enough that he is concerned that something in the river, some parasite or exotic microbe, will get into his body via this wound, and, because they are hours away from any Western medical care, he might get sick and die here. So he's chosen not to wade across the river. He's chosen to sit on the rocks of the riverbed, and wait.

The heat is extreme, and he and his Sudanese friend have been biking for hours, on and off, so the American is happy to have some time alone. But soon the American is not alone. There is a tall man wading across the river toward him, a friend of his Sudanese friend. The American fears what news this second friend could be bringing, why his friend hadn't come himself.

'Hello!' the second friend says.

The American says hello.

'Our mutual friend has sent me. He would like you to visit the village over the river. He has sent me to bring you across.'

The American tells him that he's OK, that he's fine, that he would like to stay where he is. He is embarrassed to admit that he doesn't want to wade through the water, which is knee-deep, with his small wound, so he says he's tired and would like to stay.

The second friend stands above him, flummoxed. 'Please will you come across the river with me?' he asks. 'I was given this task.'

The American explains that he's very tired and that he and their mutual friend agreed that he would stay here, on the riverbed, and that this is OK, that the second friend needn't worry.

The second friend's face is twisted, pained. 'Well, you see, in our culture,' he says, and the American winces, for these words usually precede an unpleasant request, 'we must help our guests. It's my duty to help you get to the other side.'

The American again insists that he doesn't want to or need to go across the river. As a last resort, the American shows him his wound and tries to explain the possibility that it might become infected.

'But this river is clean,' the second friend says.

'I'm sure it is,' the American says, hating himself for seeming fragile, 'but I read about the many infections we can get here, given the different microbes . . .' The second friend is looking doubtful. 'Just like if you came to the US,' the American continues. 'You would be subject to diseases that were unfamiliar to you. You could get far sicker, far quicker, than we could in our own land . . .'

The second friend shakes off all this talk. 'But in our culture,' he says again, and the American wants to yell: *This has nothing to do with your culture. You know this and I know this.* 'In our culture it is not permitted to allow a guest to sit here like this.'

The second friend continues to look pained, and the American begins to realize that the friend will be in trouble – with their mutual friend, and the mutual friend's family, and with everyone else in the town – if the second friend does not accomplish this one task of getting the American across the river. Now the second friend is looking into the distance, his hands on his hips. He squints at a fisherman who is sitting in a small dugout canoe in the bend of the river and an idea occurs to him. He goes running to the fisherman.

And soon he is back with the fisherman in tow. 'This man will take you across.'

To the American, the notion of this fisherman interrupting what he's doing to ferry him across a shallow river is worse, in so many ways, than the thought of contracting some waterborne infection. He tries to refuse again but he knows now that he's losing. He's lost.

'I don't want this,' he says.

'Please. This man will take you. You will not get wet.'

The American is smiling grimly, apologetically, at the fisherman, who is not happy to have been asked to do this. *No one wants this*, the American wants to say to the second friend, *no one but you*. But now, because the fisherman is waiting, and the second friend has gone to such trouble, it seems the path of least resistance is to get into the canoe and go across the river. So the American gets in, and notices that in the canoe are six inches of water, so he doesn't sit, but only squats among a few nets and no fish.

The fisherman has nowhere to sit, so he stands in the water, and begins to pull the canoe across the river in long, laboured strides. The second friend is walking next to the fisherman and the two of them argue loudly in Dinka about what's happening. The fisherman is clearly annoyed that this American needs to be ferried across the river like some kind of despot and the second friend is likely saying *I know, I know, Lord knows I know*. And the two of them are forming, or confirming, an idea of this American and all Westerners: that they will not walk across a shallow river, that they insist on commandeering canoes from busy fishermen and being pulled across while they squat inside. That they are afraid to get wet.

But the American did not want to go across the river at all. He did not ask for this. He did not ask for any of this. All he wants is to be a man sitting on a riverbed. He doesn't want to be a guest, or a white man, or a stranger or a strange man, or someone who needs to cross the river to see anything at all. ∎

String Theory

This is the closest you can get to flight:
tugging the heartstrings of a kite
whose loops and dives remind you
of your son's handwriting, his quest
for heights. How long is the piece of string
that tethers us to this moment, you'd think.
Kissing the shuttle your mother would
suck the thread through until one day

she choked on its fibres. In the schoolyard
you stretched a cat's cradle between
raw fingers. No, you will not be
dyed in the wool, you will grasp the nettle
– the firmer the grip the less they sting.
You want to spin out this hour
forever. But you will let your son fly
to Crete to see his father. On tenterhooks

you think how string constricts, how
it connects, how you followed it back
to Rawtenstall. Your son is unravelling
the kite's cord. He cannot lip-read
your mee-maw as you try to reel him
in. If you let them go they will
come back, says the theory. Just words.
Like birds, falling into the sea.

THE HUDSON
RIVER SCHOOL

David Searcy

I'm in the dental hygienist's chair and she's a new one, although very much the same bright, cheery presence as the last, which works for me. The unencumbered heart is best, I think, in matters such as these. She seems about the age of my daughters, which I mention as we talk. She's from west Texas where her father is a rancher. I'm a writer. Well, her sister is a writer. Really. Children's books. How about that. It's a nice day. You can see downtown from here. We're on the eighth floor. I've been coming here for years – I've gone through four or five hygienists – and I've always liked the view. I think there may be something classically romantic (if that's not a contradiction) about the view and my condition as I view it. Like those grand romantic nineteenth-century landscapes so majestic you don't see at first the tiny human figure there, oblivious and engaged in tiny purposes of his own, right at the edge of where the whole world seems to fall away toward heaven. This is just like that except it's Dallas, Texas, with no place to fall away to and I'm only here for a cleaning.

When I'm able to speak again it is to lie about my flossing habits and ask about her childhood on the ranch – I spent some time on a ranch myself when I was young, pretending to help with shearing sheep and hunting the wild dogs that would prey on them. It's coyotes in west Texas, she says. And so develops out of all this bright and cheery and obligatory chit-chat in the eighth-floor dentist's office such a strange, opaque and mysterious tale it startles me and makes me ask if she'd mind if I spoke with her father about the events. It seems there occurred, a number of years ago on her father's ranch, an alarming rise in coyote depredations among his flock. The lambs, especially, suffered terribly. He believed it was the work of a single animal but his efforts to hunt it down were unsuccessful. For two seasons he tried all the usual snares and calls but nothing worked. The animal was too cunning. And the lambs continued to die. Then he hit upon a new idea – and here's the part I'd like to know a little more about and why I'd like to give him a call, find out just where the idea came from, whether he made the tape recording for the purpose, already had it, or whatever; how it felt to do what he did, if it seemed desperate or dishonourable or too risky in some indefinable way. One morning he took a tape recording of his infant daughter's cries (not those of Lila, my hygienist, but another daughter's cries – at first I thought she meant he took the child herself) out into the tall grass or the bush, the range, whatever you call it out there where the coyotes wait to take away your lambs, and played the recording as he watched with his rifle ready. And it worked. The coyote came, he shot it dead, the depredations pretty much stopped and that was that. She writes her father's name and number on the appointment card and says she's sure he wouldn't mind at all and that she'll see me in six months.

But six months later I've not called him. Though I've thought about it often enough. I've even gone online to look up Sterling City, Texas – which is the nearest town to the ranch – and used that ghostly Google Maps capability that enables you to descend from heavenly cartographic altitudes right down into the street-level world to pass among the living. I'll pass west on Fourth Street – Highway 87 – through the middle of town, which isn't much, proceeding in those spooky-smeary increments of fifty yards or so. You don't just jerk along between the discontinuous locations like you'd think. They've introduced a bit of theatre here, I guess. So when you click from one point to another along the virtual yellow stripe – from here in front of this boarded-up feed store, say, to where that little white-haired lady waits to cross the street on up the block – it all goes blurry, sweeps away to the rear like smoke in a wind before things re-materialize around the next coordinate where you find you've overshot the white-haired lady, have to spin that magic compass thing to turn around and get a closer look. She looks uncertain. She looks past you down the highway to the west where the town itself sort of blurs away into mesquite and scrub and rolling empty distances. On down the road I pause and spin the compass thing again but I can't see her. I suppose she got across. I get a sense of how it looks, though. This sort of scrubby open country. Line of hills off in the distance. I keep thinking I might spot some sheep or something – maybe a coyote even. Everything's so open. But the resolution isn't very good. Those smudges out there could be anything. A mile or two outside of town the virtual yellow stripe splits off to the left down Highway 158. I drift that way for a while until the sameness seems to settle in completely. Then I stop and look around and then I'm lost. I can't tell which is the way to go and for a second I'm like Cary Grant in *North by Northwest*, stuck out here in my business suit in the middle of nowhere, absolutely lost.

I think the view across the city from the eighth-floor examination room is better than a fish tank, although possibly to similar effect. Whatever happens here so privately and painfully, so close to the simple limits of the body, don't forget about the fish, the endless ocean where you come from and the mystery of it all in which the tears of your discomfort will dissolve before you know it. Actually, though, the view is only to the edges of downtown – another high-rise blocks the best part of the skyline – but in any case I'm back again and haven't called her father. And perhaps she's just a little disappointed, having told him I might do so. I apologize, explaining how terrifically tangled up I've managed to get in my current project, but I really had the time and should have called. There's something here that makes me hesitate.

Back home I open my little kit and toss the floss away, replace my orange toothbrush with a green one. Later on I'm paused on Highway 87 at the edge of Sterling City once again for no particular reason, gazing past the brown-brick church and the service station out to where it all just fades away to open country. It's a nice day here as well. The blue sky hazes into white near the horizon. It's late morning,

I would guess. My girlfriend, Nancy, a painter who pays very close attention to the way things look and has lived in California where they know what coyotes look like, says she saw one near my house once. Right out here in these densely ordinary 1950s neighbourhoods one foggy night quite late. It stood in the grass beneath the power lines that run beside the tollway. She had come across the Northaven Bridge and there it was, just standing there long-legged in the grass in the foggy pale pink tollway light. She stopped and rolled her window down for a better look. And for a moment it looked back, then loped away.

A number of years ago on Forest Lane, not half a mile from here, in very heavy afternoon traffic, I encountered a giant snapping turtle trying to cross the road. And it had almost made it somehow, crossing all six lanes, but found itself unable to mount the kerb. I parked my car to block the traffic, got behind it, trying to keep away from the bloody but still dangerous-looking beak – it might have been injured by a car or just from bashing against the kerb – but anyway this thing was big around as a trash-can lid and weighed about fifty pounds, so it was all I could do to hoist it over the kerb and sort of point it toward a narrow grassy corridor that ran behind some houses. There was no place in the area I could think of that might call to such a creature. No place anywhere nearby for it to have come from. But next morning it was gone. I've seen raccoons at night dart in and out of storm sewers on my street. And once, alerted by the yelps and exclamations of my neighbour who was fighting to control her dog, a toad the size and volume of a mixing bowl right out there in the gentle summer evening in the street beneath the street lamp. I encouraged it – one sort of stomps and lunges – out of the street into another neighbour's yard. Then we retreated – she with her wild-eyed dog and I with my thoughts. That toad was even bigger than the giant African bullfrogs I had seen at the Dallas Zoo. It had no business here. Nor anywhere we care about, where limits are imposed and children sleep and dream unburdened by outrageous possibilities. In the morning, though, of course, it too was gone. Where in the world do these things come from? Is the city like a net? Does our imagination – urban, grid-like – drag behind us deeper than we know? And these are just the ones we see. Or are they simply passing through? Our world perhaps a little ghostly to them, streets and houses hardly here at all, a sort of blur like smoke across an older landscape.

I can't find the appointment card with Lila's father's name and number on it. Which, I imagine, lets me off the hook for a while. But then, a day or two later, there it is tucked into my wallet. 'Lila King, RDH' on the front and on the back, across a gauzy reproduction of three vaguely post-impressionistic apples, 'Courtney King' and two phone numbers, cell and home. It isn't *that* King Ranch, though. That south-Texas nation state with a line of fancy pickup trucks named after it. I made sure. So I just call him. What the hell.

He's on the highway in his pickup truck – a good old honest pickup truck I'll bet. And he remembers being told that I might call. And I can't tell, at first, how this is going to go. I like his voice. That broad and easy, pure west-Texas way of speaking that I like to think is somehow fundamental, undistorted, like the structure of a crystal that's had adequate room to form. If I attempt to imitate it – try to demonstrate and let myself get into that west-Texas sort of talk, which is the way all Texans probably ought to talk and maybe did before the cities pinched our noses and our vowels – I find it hard to stop. I find I want to be the one who speaks like that, regards the world that way. Whatever way that is. I think he seems OK with this. Amused a little, maybe. We'll just drive on down the highway – is it 87? I will wonder later – and he'll tell me how it happened, how the whole thing really happened over a very long period of time, a generation in fact between his tape recording of his infant daughter's cries and rediscovering them and taking them out there with him up to higher ground – a 'mountain' as he calls it – maybe sixty miles away where he would spend the night and 'come down from on top' at the crack of dawn – that's how he says it; he decided he would 'come down from on top'.

I'm checking my notes and they don't tell me why it was sixty miles – I'll have to ask him later. Maybe they lived away from the ranch then, or the coyote had been spotted somewhere else – but anyway this draws it out somehow. Reveals, it seems to me, more clearly something about the strangeness of it. Travelling such a distance with that tape recording, taking it so far away. The boom box or who knows – I guess it could have been an older reel-to-reel; I'll have to ask about that, too – but I imagine it beside him in the pickup truck that evening, and this daughter, this same one, Joellen, seventeen now, out on a date that night, I think he said. She was waiting for her date and he had come across this tape a little earlier and his wife said, 'Why not use it? Why not use that tape and see if it comes to that?' As if, somehow, their daughter waiting there so beautifully, I'm sure, and maybe vulnerably as well, brought this to mind. This possibility. But he's heading away that evening, taking all that with him there on the seat beside him in a way (I shouldn't give my imagination so much room, I know, details are bound to shift), but there beside him, surely, something to consider as pertaining to the squalling, fragile origins of things. Not to discuss with himself or anything like that but there beside him nonetheless. A hunter's mind, a rancher's mind, you'd think, would have to have a certain peripheral vision, as it were – and maybe that is what you hear in those long, slow, inflected vowels between the consonants, like wind between the fence posts, that provisional sense of things not quite in view. OK, too much. But still – how many lambs had died? He said two 'crops'. Two years – two crops. All lost, I guess. I hate to think of how many fleecy, squalling lambs two crops might be. My uncle Jack, who oversaw that ranch near Glen Rose where I spent time in my teens, ascribed to sheep a strangely maladaptive fatalism whereby, merely nipped by the predator, barely marked, not really harmed at all, they'd drift into a kind of shock or resignation, fail to eat and finally die. My uncle Jack was more a hunter and outdoorsman, not a rancher. So who knows? Another thing I need to ask about. But I remember one time having to kill a lamb or kid we found near death – a little mark where he'd been bitten on his hind leg. That was all. It makes the wild dog or the coyote or the wolf a kind of metaphor to sheep. It's the approach that counts. The fact of it. The terrible apparition.

So, Lila's father spends the night up there on the mountain with the tape-recorded cries and in the morning 'at the crack of dawn' comes down and sets it up. He turns it on low and lets it play for about three minutes, and I think this is what interests me the most. How was the light? Was it one of those hazy dawns with redness spreading all along the edge of things but not yet casting shadows so it's hard to pick out movement in the distance? Did it take him back to mornings when they'd hear the baby squalling, have to get up in the chill to attend to her, never dreaming this would happen – that those cries might drift away like this, uncomforted across the empty landscape? That's the worst thing that could happen. And yet here he is. He turns it up a notch. And then, not thirty seconds later, out of the lifting gloom, the coyote making for him at a dead run. Does he comprehend the risk? What if he misses? There's no end to it then. The lambs will die. The cries go on and on. But at a hundred yards he drops him. Pow. One shot from a .280 Remington with a seven-power scope. The world continues and he pays Joellen the two hundred dollars he promised. She and the next year's lambs grow up. And there you have it. It was an old one, he says. A smart one. You could tell by the old snare scars. But not very big – maybe thirty-five pounds – which he thought odd. He has the skull and the hide at home.

I hate to floss. It seems sort of prissy – like a manicure or something. But I know I really should. My girlfriend flosses all the time. I can't see Lila's father flossing, though. A toothpick, sure. But flossing? I don't know. How we attend ourselves seems touchy, somehow, out here in the open. Out on the range, the scrub, the prairie or whatever, where a sharp peripheral eye is so important. One's attention should be outwardly directed. I remember on Nantucket once we visited the seventeenth-century Jared Coffin House. The oldest house on the island, I believe. It's near the centre of town but up a little rise surrounded by trees so it's not hard to imagine the isolation back when it was new. It's one of those massive-chimneyed, tiny-windowed post-medieval houses so protective, so much more concerned with warmth than light, you sense a certain built-in trepidation. There's a clear, mown yard around it and a chain across the simple open door with a sign announcing times for tours. It's like the houses children draw. It's like the first house in the world. An upstairs bedroom with a cradle by a window breaks your heart. A tiny window in the heavy white-painted planking of the wall above the ancient hooded cradle with a corner of its little quilt turned back. The bed next to it is completely made, its antique quilt pulled up, a single pillow placed on top. We know they're gone, these people, centuries ago. It's just that cradle's little quilt turned back, receptive still as if to make us think the child's still here somewhere, that maybe there's a chance she's not quite lost, that someone still might bring her, stand there by the window in the evening for a moment holding all that's close and dear while gazing out upon what must have seemed, in 1680-something in the New World, such a terrifying gulf. And for a moment simply standing there, the child presented to it. What has this to do with flossing? you may ask. Well, something, surely.

Now that I'm into it I should call him again. To let him know I'm serious. That I've had to put the book aside for a while and now there's time. So it's been – what? Almost a year. And I should let him know I'd like to come and visit. Nancy too. She'd love to come. He seemed OK with that before. It's taken this long just to start and then to figure out which way it's going to go. I ring him up. And once again there seems to be a little hesitation right at first but then it's very easy, very friendly – sure, he'd love for us to come. They have a couple of extra rooms, and no, the last motel in Sterling City closed four years ago. But we should come. He'll take me varmint hunting, take down that .280, which he hasn't fired since back there on that hillside on that morning. We should come to see the wild flowers, too. They're everywhere. There's been a lot of rain and now they're everywhere and not just blue bonnets either – he can get a little tired of just the blue bonnets – but the other kinds as well, the Indian paintbrush and the others, lots of red and pink and yellow. It's spectacular right now.

I don't get back to him till February, though. Somehow. A year again almost. Or I guess I did call once but it was very brief and he was busy; grandkids coming. And by then I'd got all caught up in the novel once more, trying to find the end and taking longer than I'd hoped – an unproductive trip abroad took time, and more time to reveal itself as altogether useless to the project. It's a thing I seem to do – write past, way past sometimes, the proper endings of things. I hope that's not what's happening here. It's hard to tell, though, when you're not so sure what you're up to in the first place. At the very least I'd like to get some photographs of him. Joellen, maybe, if she's around. And of the coyote skull of course. The countryside. And the location where it happened. Anyway, it's February and I see I've got a dental check-up scheduled for the end of the month and figure maybe now is the time to call. Maybe there's a process here or something. I'll say, Lila, spoke to your dad again, and that will take the conversation out into the emptiness, the edge of the world, the prairie where I'd rather be in any case. I catch him puttering around in the garage. It's cold. They've had a little snow. There is an echo to his voice but otherwise it's just the same. A little slow at first. I tell him bet you thought you had escaped. But no, that's fine. He's glad to talk. And so we do – about all sorts of things. How I'd like Nancy to do a sketch of the skull if that's OK. Of course it is. He has the hide as well. The pelt. Whatever you call it. I remember. He says hide, I think. A red-tinged one. Your bounty used to get docked for that, he says. Red-tinged, red-tinted. They prefer the lighter-coloured ones. The red ones come from the east. It makes good collar fur for jackets, though there's not much market for it any more. I like the thought of red-tinged coyotes drifting down from the east, through cities even, ordinary neighbourhoods, as silent as the butterflies that come through in the fall. I'm thinking next month, if the weather's nice, might be a good time to come. He thinks so too. And stay in San Angelo maybe, just to keep things flexible. That's not too far. But anyway I'll call.

It's getting close to my appointment so I guess it's time to floss. So I can say oh every now and then. Not regularly. But now and then. You know. I've got this implement. A sort of toothbrush handle with the earnest ergonomics of a target pistol grip and at whose working end is a little plastic bow strung with about an inch of floss. These little bow-and-floss assemblies are disposable and subtle and ingenious, with the floss acquiring tension as the bow snaps into a complicated socket so configured as to provide a perfect lock-up as the limbs of the bow compress with normal use, but to release when they are pressed against a surface. It has counter-intuitive angles. Asymmetrical rubber inserts. It's as if designed by NASA to anticipate all difficulties. All extremes of temperature and atmosphere. Uncertainty, indifference. I have had it a while and tried it once or twice. And I imagine even lying there unused it must have prophylactic properties. And yet I do not love it. I regard it with suspicion and regret. It's unbecoming, I've decided. So, what makes it unbecoming? Do you think the little birds that clean the teeth of crocodiles are unbecoming? No, of course not. I'm OK with little birds.

The elevator in my dentist's office building has a glass wall that invites you to appreciate the view on your way up. For the first few floors you're shown the parking garage, but five and above you're looking over buildings, trees and neighbourhoods and then clear out to the skyline – unobstructed here, the whole expanse of downtown east to west, though in the morning haze it flattens into blurry grey like mountains. Lila's hair has changed from bright and cheery blonde to serious brown. I think the seriousness is natural. She spent two weeks, I believe she said, as a volunteer in Africa providing dental services. A pot of boiling water for sterilization. She was amazed at all the things she took for granted. Spoke to your dad again, I tell her. And we talk about west Texas and the distance and the drive – not bad, she says. Five hours maybe if you stop for lunch. She shows me on her phone – I'm still astonished at these phones – a couple of photos. One, a pencil sketch her father did of a French bulldog – the kind she's always loved. He has an artistic side that pops out and surprises now and then, she says. The other is an old school yearbook photo that she calls his Hollywood shot. And so it is. That deep-eyed, square-jawed sort of handsome that can seem a little menacing. This time it's a pretty easy session. All checked out and ready to go before I know it. Not a word about the flossing. It's still early. You can see the haze still hanging over the city. There's a smoky-looking layer at the horizon. She presents me with a little plastic bag of dental-hygienic odds and ends. When I get home I'll toss the floss and keep the toothbrush. It's a green one this time. That's good. I don't care for orange.

It seems that inch or two of snow they got last month was it. They're edging into drought. They've got the red-flag warnings up, he says. No rain. Just wind. And dry as it can be. And once a fire gets going there is not a whole lot you can do. But sure, come on. Just give me a call, he says. I'll meet you on the highway. Bring some rain.

We leave the interstate at Cisco and head south on Highway 206 – a very narrow, uneventful road which feels, to Nancy, like we've touched down from some altitude into the actual world. And I imagine it's like Google Maps to her – the way she dozes, waking now and then from smoky, smeary dreams along the virtual yellow stripe to look about. Where are the animals? she wonders at one point. She means wild animals like deer. It's open country and you'd think there might be something other than cattle to be glimpsed out there among the scrub and scrubby-looking trees. We stop at a Dairy Queen in Cross Plains. I love Dairy Queens. You hardly see them any more except out in the wilderness. A sort of consolation. You're allowed a chocolate malt – or that elaborate Oreo-cookie and ice-cream thing that Nancy likes – because you're out here at the edge of things where love grows thin and dust (or smoke – I'm not sure which) is blowing down the street. A very small and old and bent (and, I can't help but think, combustible-looking) man walks in on what appears to be a regular errand to receive, across the counter from a girl who calls him Paw Paw, lunch all boxed and ready to go. To take to Mamaw, he announces. Nothing for him. It's Mamaw's lunch. Does he not feel well? Probably not. He stands outside and waits to cross the street. I'm thinking what if the Google Maps survey vehicle were to drive by at this moment with its panoramic camera. Then he's caught like that poor white-haired lady. Standing there in the blowing dust with Mamaw's lunch forever. Mamaw waiting. Hope departing in the red-flagged afternoon.

I spent some time in San Angelo once when I was little but I don't remember this part north of Highway 67 where it all goes sort of flat and indistinct. The Chicken Farm Art Center Bed and Breakfast doesn't proclaim itself. No flashing neon rooster in a nightshirt and beret like you'd expect. Rather, it seems to disappear out here, submerge into the natural loss of clarity and category. Just the way things tend to run together as they fade out into prairie, which I think is what you see, or certainly sense, as a kind of emptiness down there at the end of the street. We take it slowly; let the spirit voices guide us.

It's all here though. Even a restaurant they've installed in an old feed silo. And what must have been hen-houses given over to the artists and the craftsmen and their products, which appear to issue forth about as happily and easily as those of the former residents. There are available rooms. A couple of importuning cats. It's pretty active on the weekends, we are told. But this is Monday. Not much going on. In the courtyard there are glass-top tables here and there opacified by a layer of dust. There's been a lot of dust, our hostess says. We get the Santa Fe Room, a poster of a painting of a pueblo scene confirms. It's from an Arizona gallery Nancy showed in very briefly years ago. The cats are out there all night long. Sometimes we hear them at the window.

In the morning they have joined me – Nancy takes a little longer – at the table I have dusted off to share my blueberry scone, which is the breakfast part of the bed-and-breakfast deal, and help me wait till nine o'clock when I've decided I should call. I am reluctant. I think maybe I'm imposing way too much on this whole thing. A pretty simple, even delicate sort of thing. But come on out, he says. I scribble down directions. He will meet us at the turn-off.

Nancy loves to travel anywhere. Especially on exploratory missions where you get to take your time and look around. And look around is what there is to do out here. Your eye goes way out to the hazy edge of things. You're like a panoramic camera. The periphery is everything. When she and I first met, I told her stories of how Dallas used to be. How, in the sixties, you could drive north past the edge of it and find yourself in farmland, open country. Now, of course, you can't. The city and the suburbs have expanded and there isn't any north edge any more, although I told her we might try to find a remnant if she'd like. And so we did. It took an afternoon – like trying to find a childhood scar that's drifted across the body over the years. And it wasn't much. No more than twenty acres, near some railroad tracks, that seemed to have been under cultivation until recently, or maybe just a haying field – I think there was a tractor under some trees. But we got out and all around you heard the traffic and we thought, well, this is it, the ancient shoreline where the Greeks made camp outside the walls of Troy, where you could stand and gaze upon the empty world.

We get to the turn-off but we're early. He's not here yet. So we park just off the highway next to the white caliche road that leads dead straight out into nothing as if that were its intention. We get out. It seems like how the world must look when you're not looking. Settled back to fundamentals. Like that Englishman who, awakened in the middle of the night, will have no accent, speaks like anybody else. I find a .270 Winchester cartridge case on the ground and show it to Nancy. Somebody must have spotted a deer, I guess. She holds it to her ear. What are you doing? She is listening to it whistle in the wind. I want a picture of the road before he comes. Before a cloud of dust suggests there's something out there after all. Right now it makes a perfect diagram. Just three lines. Just dry grass and chalky road straight to the horizon. That's three lines, three colours – brown and white and blue. A tiling pattern. Or a good state flag, I think. The wind implicit. It would flutter in its own implicit breeze. It makes it hard to hold the camera steady. It's like a periscope. I've resurfaced. A huge dark pickup truck has pulled in off the highway. Not the way I was expecting. Cloud of dust as he emerges – massive, smiling, cowboy-hatted, grey-goateed, tooled leather suspenders. Later Nancy will decide he has Roy Rogers eyes. She always loved Roy Rogers and that squinty, soft amusement in his eyes. I'm going to say the English actor Oliver Reed – though Oliver Reed awakened suddenly in the middle of the night because the cows are loose or something and he hasn't time to change into an Englishman. My hand is gripped, enveloped, and within about a minute I am offered chewing tobacco – which I actually consider for a second as a test I'm likely to fail – and then a nickel-plated, lavishly engraved Colt .44 for our protection. I believe Roy's having fun. But I don't care. It's nice engraving. Not as good as factory, though, he says. It'd be worth more with factory engraving. Here we go. I run to the car to get my hunting knife. A good one too. Handmade with a nice stag grip. So, see? I'm armed. And rather stylishly in fact. We follow him out the white caliche road to nowhere. Nancy's laughing. And they're both such beautiful weapons, dear. Shut up, I try to explain. No, you shut up. No, you shut up.

It's a large and handsome limestone house on top of a hill. A little brown dog named Scout is running around and trying to make its yapping heard above the wind. The wind is steady. There's nothing out here to discourage or inflect it. You can see the distant hazy edge of everything from here. And then so strangely way out there to the north and west and barely emergent from the haze (I think they use a haze-grey paint) as if belonging to those fundamental properties of things you never see except when things reduce like this to fundamentals are the giant wind turbines, the really huge ones with the football-field-long blades. So that's where the wind comes from, you'd think, if you didn't know. Of course, it has to come from somewhere.

Everything up here on top of the hill is new. They built the house about four years ago. The heavy, limestone-founded, iron-railed fence. And, so precariously it seems, on a lower terrace on the west side near the fence where the hill drops suddenly away, a beautiful playground for the grandkids. Tent-roofed structures – we would

Take the trip

Have *Granta* delivered to your door
four times a year and save up
to 38% on the cover price.

Subscribe now by completing the form overleaf, visiting granta.com
or calling UK free phone 0500 004 033

UK
£36 | £32 by Direct Debit

Europe
£42

Rest of the world*
£46

*Not for readers in US, Canada or Latin America

'An indispensable part
of the intellectual landscape'
— *Observer*

GRANTA.COM

GRANTA
THE MAGAZINE OF NEW WRITING

SUBSCRIPTION FORM FOR UK, EUROPE AND REST OF THE WORLD

Yes, I would like to take out a subscription to *Granta*.

GUARANTEE: If I am ever dissatisfied with my *Granta* subscription, I will simply notify you, and you will send me a complete refund or credit my credit card, as applicable, for all un-mailed issues.

YOUR DETAILS

MR / MISS / MRS / DR ....

NAME ....

ADDRESS ....

....

POSTCODE ....

EMAIL ....

☐ Please tick this box if you do not wish to receive special offers from *Granta*
☐ Please tick this box if you do not wish to receive offers from organizations selected by *Granta*

YOUR PAYMENT DETAILS

1) ☐ Pay £32 (saving £20) by Direct Debit
   To pay by Direct Debit please complete the mandate and return to the address shown below.

2) Pay by cheque or credit/debit card. Please complete below:

   1 year subscription: ☐ UK: £36   ☐ Europe: £42   ☐ Rest of World: £46

   3 year subscription: ☐ UK: £99   ☐ Europe: £108   ☐ Rest of World: £126

   I wish to pay by   ☐ CHEQUE   ☐ CREDIT/DEBIT CARD
   Cheque enclosed for £ _____ made payable to *Granta*.

   Please charge £ _____ to my: ☐ Visa   ☐ MasterCard   ☐ Amex   ☐ Switch/Maestro

   Card No. ☐☐☐☐☐☐☐☐☐☐☐☐☐☐☐☐

   Valid from *(if applicable)* ☐☐☐☐   Expiry Date ☐☐☐☐   Issue No. ☐☐

   Security No. ☐☐☐

SIGNATURE .... DATE ....

Instructions to your Bank or Building Society to pay by Direct Debit

BANK NAME ....

BANK ADDRESS ....

POSTCODE ....

ACCOUNT IN THE NAMES(S) OF: ....

SIGNED ....

DATE ....

DIRECT Debit

Instructions to your Bank or
Building Society: Please pay
Granta Publications direct debits
from the account detailed on
this instruction subject to the
safeguards assured by the direct
debit guarantee. I understand
that this instruction may remain
with Granta and, if so, details will
be passed electronically to my
bank/building society. Banks and
building societies may not accept
direct debit instructions from
some types of account.

Bank/building society account number
☐☐☐☐☐☐☐☐

Sort Code
☐☐☐☐☐☐

Originator's Identification
9 1 3 1 3 3

Please mail this order form with
payment instructions to:

Granta Publications
12 Addison Avenue
London, W11 4QR
Or call 0500 004 033
or visit GRANTA.COM

have called them forts – on stilts with slides descending, one a giant twisty yellow plastic tube. Suspended tyre. Rope-ladder rigging. And a swing set with three swings, each plastic seat a different colour – not yet faded yellow, blue and red. A choice. And then which way to face – the house across the drive just up the hill, or that great emptiness toward which the hill drops off right there not twenty feet away. To which you'd sense yourself presented every time at the top of the arc where letting go, to a child especially I imagine, always seems a possibility. In the big high-ceilinged living room are all the animals Nancy didn't see on the way down. All the ones she'd periodically wake herself to look for out in the scrub along the highway. Here they are. The biggest elk I've ever seen above the fireplace. On the floor a brown-bear rug. And on the wall across the room above the bookcase is a group of horned and antlered beasts so fully and expansively themselves they lose significance as trophies. They are specimens. All 'fair chase', though, I'm told. 'I wouldn't use a blind. That's bullshit.' And the meat, where it's appropriate, consumed. So they are cleanly, self-sufficiently here. The animal representatives. And here and there among them, family photographs. A needlepoint genealogy.

I think the newness throws me just a bit. He says his family has been ranching for a hundred years out here. And yet it's like they've just arrived. Or maybe just arrived again. To build a house like this, a big receptive house like this out here must be a different sort of undertaking. Not like in the city where the concept is established, no particular risk involved. Out here you probably need to know a lot more clearly what you're doing. How to situate yourself. You've got your basics here to deal with after all. Your wind, your emptiness, your animals, your house. He stands in the middle of the living room and looks wherever I look, seems to re-appreciate these things. One photograph I return to is a black-and-white of Courtney and his brother from the fifties, each boy posed identically dressed in cowboy hat, fleece-collared jacket, jeans and boots behind his fat prize-winning sheep. It looks like Courtney wears his older brother's jeans, the cuffs rolled up. It's perfect somehow. In that fragile yet momentous way some Walker Evans photographs are perfect. Courtney's brother – you can't quite make out, so must infer his freckles – grins at something off to the right beyond the field of view. While Courtney and his sheep – their faces calm and close together at the centre of the picture as he hugs her about the neck to hold her still – gaze out at us. They make an emblem against the dead white-painted clapboard barn behind. I take a picture of the picture. Of the elk. The other creatures on the walls. A massive grizzly skull he shows me. And at some point – I had hoped to wait for this I think, to put it off, to try to sort of settle back into what I imagined I was doing here – he's standing there with the coyote skull. So small in all of this. A tiny thing. Like something lost and found – oh, here it is. He holds it out lightly as if it's made of glass. I hear the women in the kitchen. Lila's mother, Elaine, looks very much like Lila. In a group of Walker Evans faces she would be the pretty one. I take a picture of him standing there like that. And then a close-up. He brings out the hide. The whole thing – dangly legs and tail and everything. The superficial coyote. Like a ghost. Where are the scars? I ask. He shows me on the legs the smooth black marks left by the snares. I ask Elaine to come outside on the porch and hold it for a picture. In the wind it flaps like paper. Like it wants to blow away.

In the early nineties when this happened they lived north of here in Snyder where the girls attended school. The ranch – a lease – was sixty miles away near Silver in Coke County. Coyotes, Courtney tells me, almost always come in about the first of September. Yearlings usually, driven from other ranges. Most of these are taken with snares. This one was older. He had females with him too. A male will generally hunt with a female. They shot three of his. Each year he'd have another. After the second year he'd killed about 120 lambs. A three-pound lamb can get to ninety pounds in three and a half to four months if the range conditions are right. Sometimes a coyote waits. If there are rabbits to eat – and in those years there were; a 'surfeit', Courtney says – a coyote waits until a lamb weighs maybe twenty pounds. A lamb, of course, is easier and fatter than a rabbit but, somehow, he knows to wait. How strange to think about a coyote out there – what could be more simply, purely present than a coyote? – but a coyote out there thinking of the future as if it were just a simple thing like dust or wind or something. Nancy's sketching in the kitchen. There's good light in there. She's chatting with Elaine. The coyote skull is on the table. Courtney's brought out that .280 that he hasn't shot since then. It was a brand-new rifle, too. Except for the buttstock it's entirely camo-taped. He says he did that while he waited on that morning. Not so easy, I imagine, in the dark. We're in the living room. He's got his tools to reattach the scope, to put the rifle back together as it was. He says that third year, about the third week in April after they had gotten through with shearing, there was a perfectly calm and moonlit night so he drove to where the sheep were gathered, parked and spread his bedroll out in the back of the pickup truck, lay down and waited. It was midnight probably, maybe a little later, when he heard the coyote howling. It was very still and the howling was right there, 'like right up on you'. Then the sheep began to run and bleat and he raised up with his rifle in the moonlight but no coyote. He had taken what he wanted. After that they pulled the lambs off the ewes and put them in the feedlot to protect them and that worked pretty well for the lambs but then the coyote went for the ewes.

Andrew Delbanco, in *The Puritan Ordeal*, attempts to understand the Puritans' sense of evil in the New World. How it changed. How, in the emptiness they found here, it condensed out of that vapour they'd imagined as the absence, the 'privation', of the good into a thing, an actual presence. It's as if in such uncertainty, such emptiness, they needed more than anything to situate themselves securely opposite the danger. Had to sacrifice a bit of hope for that. And place themselves, perhaps a little more deliberately, in the world. I like to imagine the Jared Coffin House brand new. On that little hill above Nantucket a couple of generations after what seems to have been a sort of spiritual discouragement. Its newness still expressive of the general arrival, I should think. The tiny trepidatious windows peeking out upon the dark. Late in the book, Delbanco quotes the Romanian religious historian Mircea Eliade who notes that 'any village anywhere *is* the "Centre of the World"'. And by extension any house. I ask Elaine at one point, 'Doesn't it get lonely?' 'No,' she answers almost before I get the question out. It doesn't. It gets late, though. Light comes in at a softer angle. Afternoon is wearing on and I've not asked to see the tape. I'm not really sure I want to hear it. All the tapes are kept together in a little top drawer of a dresser in the guest room. All the predator-calling tapes. I hadn't realized. But certainly that makes sense. Why should you have to be a musician, as it were, with horns and squeakers or whatever? – though he uses those as well. But sure, why not just get a recording of what you want? And what you want is very specific forms of misery. I look through them: Chicken Hen Squalls, Grey Fox Distress, Young Turkey Distress, Mad Crows, Raccoon Fight, Baby Crying (Joellen). Really. There with the mad crows and the others. These things happen after all. These small misfortunes. Raccoons fight and babies cry. It's touching, though – the parenthetical attribution. Almost reluctant. He knows very well he's placed her in that range of possibilities. That the coyote doesn't care – he's looking way beyond the personal. So it's not 'Joellen Crying'. That would not be parallel. But still – as if to say I know, I know. He's got the player, too. Or not the one he used back then but one just like it. Dusty, scuffed black-box-like evidence recovered from a crash site. In the kitchen Nancy's finishing a sketch – a very nice one on grey paper. Simple side view. Charcoal pencil with white highlights. Courtney takes a seat and places the recorder on the table. 'Want to hear it?' He leans back. He has a toothpick in his mouth. See? What did I tell you? There's no flossing. There are no flossing habits here. But here? I'm thinking. Should we really play it here? Right here in the kitchen? In the fading afternoon? Elaine is standing. No expression. 'Sure,' says Nancy. What is there about the toothpick? As he gazes down. The thoughtlessness. Or no, it isn't thoughtlessness. My God. It's like a shock. I sort of expected a little accidental background noise or something. A little preparatory blankness. But it's right there. Fully present. Six weeks old I think they said. A shriek to take your breath away. The way a baby shrieks to end all shrieks – all shrieks contained therein, all forms of misery, the wilderness itself. Elaine has backed away. Of course the coyote came. How could it not. It's all right there. And it goes on and on. I'm looking at Elaine. OK. She hears her baby out there in the wilderness, I'm thinking. But it's not quite that. He shuts it off and looks at her. 'Oh my,' says Nancy. 'What?' he says. Or maybe I say, 'What?' Elaine says, 'Why didn't you pick her up?' She's gone right past the coyote. Back to the baby at that moment. 'Why did you let her cry?' 'I didn't.' Courtney smiles. 'She wouldn't stop.' She knows, of course. They know all that. So I just go ahead and ask the thing I want to ask, insert the big idea where it won't fit, I'm pretty sure, where it seems awkward and impractical – and Courtney's so polite, they're both so kind to let us come in here like this so he just listens to me, smiley-eyed, as I get all jacked up to make him see what must have been there in his heart, the faint suspicion on that morning on the hillside as he played that tape that something more was going on. He had to sense it, right? That there was something more at risk. You know. Perhaps there were misgivings. Sure, he knows. Roy Rogers knows. 'Hell, no,' he says. 'I wanted to kill it.'

There has been, along with the drought, the wind and the constant threat of fire, another hovering concern. Just after Christmas a young girl disappeared not far from here in Colorado City. Courtney's eleven-year-old granddaughter lives near there. It was believed at first that the girl, thirteen, had run away from home. But pretty soon it began to look like an abduction. Attention turned to the mother and her younger live-in boyfriend. There were reports of child pornography and drugs. Failed polygraph tests. I'm not even sure in what connection this came up. I guess we were talking, Courtney and I – Elaine and Nancy had gone off by themselves somewhere – about the coyote and the tape. About that ranch they had back then – and which I wish it had been possible to visit and is out that way, just down the road from Colorado City. It was on his mind. On everybody's mind, I guess. The miles between these little towns seem so completely empty, like a vacuum, no resistance to events, so when a fire pops up or someone disappears it's like it's right here, right outside. So people talk about the danger, what to watch for. There are certain things he told me. Not just things like don't get into cars with strangers. But more subtle things. For example, if you hear the water running after dark, don't go outside. They'll cut your water line to make you come outside. Or if you hear a baby crying. Even that. They'll do that, too. The very same thing. To bring a woman out. A girl. 'They will go out to that,' he said. Can you imagine? What if you heard that crying out there in the dark? Not even thinking of the danger – just the emptiness of that. In every sense. No parenthetical attribution there, for sure. No hope at all. Do not go out. That child is lost. Like running water. Irretrievable. Like the wind and smoke and threat of fire and everything. You can't do any good.

After he killed it, Courtney waited about a week then went out calling just to make sure. Just to see what might turn up. I should have asked what kind of call he used – I'm sure he's got all kinds. It could have been a blade of grass for all I know. Anyway, he's out there calling – out in the bush, the range; out where the coyotes wait and listen – and he's out there quite a while but nothing comes. Until, at last, a little grey fox shows up – this sounds just like a fable but it's not. This little grey fox comes skidding up within five feet or so. Starts barking at him. Barks and barks. And this is good, thinks Courtney. Coyotes tend to kill or run the foxes off. So this is good. No coyotes. Just this little fox that keeps on barking at him. Courtney grabs a handful of dust and throws it at him. Fox just backs away and keeps on barking. I didn't know a fox could bark. But this one does and won't go away. And as he tells me I keep seeing this, imagining it, as if from a certain distance. From a certain elevation as from a prominence somewhere, with Courtney standing way out there in the middle of nowhere and this little grey fox just barking. From this distance very faintly. Barking and barking. And that puff of dust dispersing in the wind. ∎

A RATIONALIST
IN THE JUNGLE

Héctor Abad

TRANSLATED FROM THE SPANISH BY ANNE MCLEAN

Feverish and Adrift

The first thing I felt when I returned from the jungle was a paralysis of willpower. I didn't shower, stayed in bed dozing, staring into space, remembering the rivers and streams I'd swum in and the places where I'd slept in Vaupés. I still felt like I was rocking in my hammock in the perpetual dusk of the longhouses, or *malocas*. Suddenly I began to tremble, to have shivers, aching bones and finally fever: a ferocious, erratic fever, along with copious sweating, sensitivity to light, burning skin and an inability to open my eyes or move.

Then, lying in bed, I remembered Martín von Hildebrand's cheerful warning: 'If you don't accept everything they offer, you might offend the shaman and he could put a curse on you.' And I clearly saw in my memory that night in the San Miguel *maloca*, when Yebá-Boso (after I had twice turned down his gourd of rancid *chicha*) approached holding two bird-bone straws in a V-shape. He piled a greyish powder on one end. Then he bent over my face and introduced the little bone tube into my left nostril. Without warning he blew hard into the other end. I felt a jolt in my head that nearly knocked me over, as if I'd had wasabi shot directly into my brain. I coughed and writhed, but courtesy demanded I offer the other nostril. Another tremendous thump to the middle of my cranium. It must have been at this moment – my delirious mind decided – that the curse of the illness entered my body.

Ten days before, I had arrived in the Amazon jungle with the best guide anyone who wants to penetrate Colombia's most remote indigenous territories could have: the anthropologist Martín von

Hildebrand. Born sixty-nine years ago in New York, the son of a Bavarian father and an Irish mother, he came to live in Bogotá at the age of six. His accent is Bogotano, but his nationality is multiple and cosmopolitan: he has a Colombian identity card, a Swiss passport and three others as well. He speaks fluent French from the schools he attended, impeccable English from New York and Dublin (where he went to university); he can get by in a few indigenous languages, and knows German from his father's side of the family, Bavarians who in spite of being Aryans and Catholic converts had to escape Nazi persecution due to the furious articles that his grandfather – the theologian Dietrich von Hildebrand – wrote against Hitler and *Mein Kampf.*

Hildebrand embarked on his first trip to Vaupés in 1971, forty years ago, and since then his life and that of the Colombian Amazon have been like two lianas intertwining, or rather like one liana that creeps over and embraces the trunk of an age-old tree every which way. He and his odd friendship with Virgilio Barco, president of the republic in the late 1980s (they used to spend hours together in the government palace, both in perfect silence), are the reason that Colombia has the most extensive indigenous *resguardos*, protected collective territories, in the world, much larger than those of Canada, Brazil or Australia. These *resguardos* are a country within a country, the size of Great Britain.

But forty years ago, even Hildebrand needed a guide to introduce him to the confusion of the jungle. His was the anthropologist Gerardo Reichel-Dolmatoff (who would later become his father-in-law). Back then Reichel was passionate about the shamanistic cultures of the Pirá Paraná River in Vaupés, and recommended Hildebrand go there. But before he ventured into the jungle for the first time Reichel gave Hildebrand five pieces of advice: 1. have his appendix removed, 2. take a first-aid course, 3. not to buy a gas-powered motor – as he'd planned – but paddle and walk, 4. never to carry his own rucksack on his back; hire indigenous porters to carry it on long hikes through the jungle, and 5. have a conversation with Monsignor Belarmino Correo, apostolic vicar in Mitú, a sort of auxiliary bishop of what was then called the *Comisaría* or Precinct of Vaupés.

Three days after his conversation with Reichel, Hildebrand no longer had an appendix (a doctor friend removed it for free) and a week later he was in the Villavicencio Hospital suturing the wound of a man who'd been bitten on the ankle by a pig. A month in the emergency ward gave him excellent first-aid skills, a brief apprenticeship that would stand him in good stead for the rest of his life.

A few weeks later Hildebrand was with the indigenous communities in the southern Vaupés region. That contact would change his life forever, and, in some way, would also determine the future and independence of the indigenous peoples of the Colombian Amazon. For better or for worse, if someone is responsible for the fact that these indigenous communities have not integrated into twentieth-century Colombian history, or the modernity of the world, that person is Martín von Hildebrand. For better rather than for worse, they are not peasant farmers, not coca growers, not missionaries, not guerrilla fighters or soldiers or servants or workers or paramilitaries; instead they are themselves. And for better or for worse, they live according to their own traditions, including the medical, hygienic and magic practices of the shamans, for me as absurd and harmful as the medical and magic practices of Catholic priests.

Martín von Hildebrand is and isn't one of them. Neither a spiritual guide nor a political leader, he seems more like a giant ear that moves up and down much of the Colombian Amazon region, listening and recommending steps to take in order to get what the people want. And what they want, most of all, is to keep their territory intact. When he is with them, he lives as they do; he's one of them, though his skin is fairer, covered in freckles from too much sun. Hildebrand has integrated into their culture comfortably. He says he follows their dietary and medical practices successfully, including high doses of *mambe* (coca leaves crushed with cecropia leaf ash) and sporadic cleanses with *yagé* and other sacred plants. If so, he hasn't done badly. In forty years of travels in the jungle, Hildebrand has never been seriously ill; he's never suffered from malaria, beriberi or dysentery. He's never been bitten by a horsefly or a snake. Nothing. He eats their thick spicy stews with a hearty appetite. Almost seventy years old, he's as strong and healthy as an Amazonian tree and slips very easily from an animated garrulousness to the most impenetrable silence. I watch him rise at dawn to do t'ai chi, then go with him to the river and we jump in naked, with one hand over our private parts ('Indigenous style,' he explains, and I tell him it seems more like 'missionary style'), like someone who baptizes himself each day with a complete immersion in the dark and sinuous waters of the Pirá Paraná.

The Famous River

Colombia is, in a certain sense, such a young country that it is still covered in forests, as the whole world was not so many millennia ago, as Europe was until a few centuries ago. However, although close to half of Colombia's territory is jungle, the majority of Colombians live far from the rainforests, up in our Andean cities, avoiding the heat and humidity, the tropical diseases, insects and snakes. The jungle is the other, another faraway country, attractive, unsettling and repellent at the same time. In the jungle most of the coca that has made us sadly notorious is grown; in the jungle the guerrillas and drug traffickers move and hide; in the jungle hostages languish; in the jungle live the least contaminated remnants of our autochthonous populations; and in the jungle lies most of our biological diversity and wealth.

Before embarking on my journey to the Pirá Paraná region, I knew nothing of this important Colombian river; I knew that down in the south almost all places had strange names 'always with the accent on the last syllable', as the poet José Eustasio Rivera said, but nothing more. The river (black or red depending on the day's light, crystal clear in the palm of your hand, wide, fast-flowing, alternately torrential or tranquil) runs from north to south, through the Department of

Vaupés, and in the middle of its course it crosses the equator before flowing into the Apaporis River – which feeds into the Caquetá, which flows into the Amazon, in Brazil by then. To get there we have to fly to Mitú, perhaps the most militarized regional capital in Colombia since November 1998 when the guerrillas took the town and held it for a whole week. And in Mitú we hire an old light aircraft, the kind that coughs and splutters and sometimes sneezes in mid-air, the kind without a single functioning needle on the control panel, that flies south for almost an hour until the pilot finds, just with the naked eye and in the middle of the swamp, the rudimentary runways along the length of the river, beside some of the indigenous settlements.

In the front seat of the small plane, beside the pilot, is Edward, a giant Englishman, two metres tall, Oxford graduate, a new species of twenty-first-century benevolent explorer, a sharp observer of our idiosyncrasies, who's writing a book about his impressions of Colombia. In the back are Martín and myself. Due to the weight of the passengers, we've had to leave behind in Mitú half of our luggage (my tins of food, gasoline for the canoe's outboard motor, extra clothes, bottles of drinking water). After a bumpy landing on the stones and little mounds of earth, we arrange a return flight with the same pilot (nine days later, in this case) and, weather and rain permitting, on the agreed day the little plane will return. If we'd wanted to make the trip overland, through swampy patches, streams and rivers, it would have taken at least twelve exhausting days, with the help of a guide with expert knowledge of the confusing jungle trails.

Curses that are Blessings

The Colombian Amazon region has been plagued in recent decades by two of our dreadful curses: guerrillas and corruption. Fear of being recruited, attacked or kidnapped by the guerrillas has stopped land-hungry settlers from going deep into the jungle, and it's been left almost intact. Thanks to the corruption of local governments, highways and roads planned to penetrate the rainforest were never built. Those two curses have protected the region from two of the worst predators on the planet: mestizos and, especially, the white man. Another curse (drug trafficking) has also not managed to bless this part of the country with its bitter wealth: the quality of the coca cultivated by the indigenous people of this area is poor (it yields very little alkaloid). And one more curse – which is almost everywhere seen as a misfortune – the migration of the young people to cities has left here enormous expanses of territory inhabited by a few handfuls of dispersed indigenous communities where only those most attached to their customs, their traditions, their relationship to the land and their ancestral cultures have endured. The result is an immense region (the size of the British Isles, as I said) inhabited by some 40,000 people whose territory cannot be invaded, colonized, governed or exploited legally by anybody except themselves. They are the inalienable masters of the biggest and most exuberant farm on the planet, a country within another country, and seem to want to preserve it as it is – virginal, tough and secret – forever.

Mining Danger

The biggest risk to the cultural and environmental conservation of the rainforest might come from the subsoil. There is no greater danger than mining to the ecological integrity of Colombian Amazonia. With the defeat or retreat of the guerrillas, with the drug traffickers' disappointment, with the arrival of less corrupt and more efficient governments, a new type of persistent visitor has appeared in these frontier territories: geologists. From Mitú you start to notice they are legion and travel all along the rivers excavating and sending soil samples to national and international laboratories. Some of these geologists have been contracted by large mining companies to have them send rock and soil samples. At the same time these companies are doing everything possible to buy titles and rights from the government to eventually enable them to exploit the subsoil.

No matter how little there might be beneath the crust, there are companies willing to buy the rights to millions of hectares. Those titles, after all, can be resold on the international market. And with a single find of gold, silver, copper, nickel or rare minerals such as coltan, the titles rise in value exponentially. That is the greatest risk these lands and the indigenous communities face. Their leaders and chiefs know it and are preparing legal defences, with the assistance of international human rights organizations such as the Gaia Foundation. They aspire to get the government to mark out unbreachable borders around their territory so that the reserves won twenty-five years ago will not be destroyed by mining. Recently the government imposed a moratorium on the sale of land titles to these territories.

While this is happening, the communities of the Pirá Paraná continue to live almost as our ancestors must have lived 10,000 years ago. This can be seen as unforgivable backwardness, but also as commendable, a sign of vitality and sacrifice in extreme conditions; surviving in the jungle, without technology, is almost as difficult as surviving in the Arctic. They are always at the limits of survival, barely avoiding death with scarce resources, very little food, and contact with technology that is uncertain, distant, sporadic and so expensive that it's almost never available. They sow twenty varieties of cassava, seven of coca, some pineapples and plantains and not much else. They collect wild fruits and roots, depending on the time of year; they eat insects, especially ants, and hunt birds and monkeys, still using blowpipes and poisoned darts. They have axes and iron farming tools (this is the advanced technology that has served them best), and plastic tanks to collect rainwater. There is the odd rusty chainsaw – that number-one enemy of centuries-old trees – but since gasoline is extremely expensive and almost impossible to acquire, these lie neglected in huts, eaten away by smoke and damp.

The Green Desert

When the technological anomaly of the plane takes off, I feel I am going inside the past of the human race, and that if a nuclear cataclysm occurred today, or a long night as the result of a meteorite, it would be these people, capable of surviving on almost nothing (water, air, leaves, seeds, insects), of eating anything, and simply with the instinct of their eyes and hands, who would have the harsh task of repopulating the world.

Never, not even in China, had I ever felt so foreign and so far from my own world. The Amazon rainforest is an immense green desert, full of life, yes, but inhospitable and almost uninhabitable for those not born there, for someone who doesn't know how to decipher the confusing hieroglyphics of the infinity of leaves, insects, reptiles, vines, roots, trees and shrubs, so many that they blend into a chaotic accumulation, a visual noise incomprehensible to inexpert eyes. The Makuna, Edduria or Barasana languages (or others of these linguistic branches spoken there) were as familiar to me as Mandarin Chinese. There, in the heartland of the Pirá Paraná, in the south of my country, right on the equator, that political and bureaucratic entity we call Colombia is such a remote thing that there aren't even any civil servants; nor is there any army or paramilitaries, or drug traffickers, or police; no hostages or kidnappers; no priests or politicians.

You turn on the transistor radio during the day, and all you hear is static and astral whistling. There is no electricity, so moonless nights are perfectly dark; there is no amplified music (what welcome respite); no mobile phone signal; there's no salt, no sugar – no shops where you might buy sugar or salt. It's impossible to get a beer, a shot of *aguardiente* or a Coke. Of course there is no Internet or television signal. They are there, the indigenous people, the masters of the jungle, with their complex lives and ancestral culture, and that indecipherable noise of the immense biological diversity: thousands and thousands of botanical and animal species, incomprehensible and identical if one is not native or at least a botanist or biologist or entomologist. A pale-faced, near-sighted urbanite like me is nothing less than handicapped in the heart of the jungle. All book learning, all literary knowledge, is useless and laughable in this place that José Eustasio Rivera called a 'green hell' and I would call a 'green desert'.

The Community of San Miguel

San Miguel is home to three hundred souls and was founded more than half a century ago by Catholic missionaries who gave it the name of the archangel. They tell me it was Father Manuel Elorza, a black Jesuit priest, who brought the image of the archangel and opened a boarding school so the Indians could study. But more than thirty years ago a group of indigenous iconoclasts got fed up with the missionary priests. There was a basic, elemental problem, and it was that the missionary teachers began to feel attracted to the indigenous girls, and took to the very courtly and discourteous task of seducing them. Women in the jungle are a more precious resource than water or cassava, so the indigenous leaders were furious. They burned the image of the archangel, knocked down the chapel and – in order not to lose their women – decided to recover their own language as well as their old rituals and religious practices. Now they live with a syncretism that includes, among many other gods, Jesus and some Christian saints and angels, as well as their ancient deities: celestial anacondas, Yuruparí jaguars, ritual plants, ancestors, souls, sons of time (supernatural beings that communicate with us during dreams or when we take *yagé*), sacred places of pilgrimage, monkeys, macaws, pacas, trees, rapids . . .

When we arrive they take us to see the *maloca* (which is the ritual centre, the meeting place, the common dining area for events and the heart of every indigenous community). The first surprise – which seems like a hallucination – occurs at this moment. Coming out of the excessive exterior light into the semi-darkness of the *maloca*, we're dazzled to find thirteen portable computers on which a group of young men (more than twenty) and one young woman are learning to use word processing programs. They are transcribing tales of their sacred places, of the myths related to their culture and the Pirá Piraná River, of their ancestral migrations, in their own languages (they belong to different ethnic groups) and in Spanish. The computers are connected to a gas-powered generator, and two teachers from the Gaia Foundation are training the young people. They type slowly with their index fingers to transpose what they have written or drawn by hand onto the screen. The drawings of animals and sacred places are scanned and added to the text.

In San Miguel there is order and cleanliness, open spaces, a football pitch, a school and a health centre. By cultural tradition, and for reasons of survival, the communities of the Pirá Paraná are semi-nomadic, with transitory fixed settlements that shouldn't last more than twenty years. After this time the surrounding land gets exhausted. The crops are sown where the forest has been felled and the stubble burned. They plant the varieties of cassava, which are the mainstay of their diet, and the coca plants, the leaves of which the indigenous people are as attached to as to their own land. Protein comes from fishing or hunting. The rest of their food is collected, depending on the season. But land, game and fruit become scarcer the longer they stay in one place. The jungle is, in a certain sense, poor; not in diversity (there's a reason pharmaceutical companies are illegally patenting its chemical wealth), but in food. Its production – without fertilizers and insecticides, which to their culture are disgraceful – does not give enough to sustain large populations. They have to divide into groups, leave the place and go off farther away in different directions, to find virgin land, cut down the forest and sow again in fertile soil. What they leave behind needs fifteen or twenty years to recuperate, and in the meantime must not be touched.

A successful settlement like San Miguel is, therefore, a danger. The journeys to the *chagras* (small plots where each family grows their crops) have been getting longer and longer, up to a six- or seven-hour walk to get there and back with the produce. That makes life difficult, and everything too laborious. This also explains why the girls (from the ages of six to ten) stay in the town to take care of the smaller children, while the adults go to plant or harvest the cassava, on round trips that take up all the hours of daylight.

Everything in the jungle is paradoxical. A successful community turns into a danger to itself. But in San Miguel there is infrastructure to collect rainwater; there is a radio-telephone to provide information about arrivals and calamities; there is a satellite telephone too, which works on solar energy and cards that can be purchased in Mitú; they receive visits from vaccination teams and they have a refrigerator (also powered by solar panels) where they can keep antivenin serum, vaccines and other basic medicines. Leaving the settlement is leaving all this, and few wish to do so. This means that due to food shortages, tensions increase. The economy they practise (commerce is practically non-existent) is not designed for so many, or for staying still for so long. But nor is it possible to throw anyone out. That is the crossroads they find themselves at: some of them should leave, but which ones?

The peoples of the rainforest cannot follow the model of the white people's town in every way, for here there is no way to supply it: there is no commerce, no currency in circulation, no means of transportation to bring in cheap food from elsewhere, or to take away what they could produce here as goods for exchange. San Miguel is the opposite of all this. Its success is synonymous with its failure.

Benjamín's *Maloca*

While staying in San Miguel we walked to Benjamín's *maloca*, the nearest community. Martín, Edward, two indigenous guides, Ernesto Ávila and Reynel Ortega, and I went for a quick visit. The plan was to have a look around and come straight back, but a torrential rainstorm caught us there and we ended up spending long hours *mambeando* in the *maloca* waiting for the weather to clear. When we got there one of Benjamín's secretaries was, at that very moment, preparing the *mambe*. *Mambe* has a bitter taste and a sour, penetrating smell, which impregnates one's whole body. Martín and the indigenous people adore this scent, but I find it very disagreeable.

When we walked into Benjamín's *maloca* I thought they were making some rhythmic music with a strange percussion instrument: a kind of cylindrical drum the length of a cannon. They put a long stick into its mouth and were banging it. The sound was rhythmical with variations: fast, slow, a very fast drum roll as a finale. The secretary pulled out the stick and examined the end covered in pieces of palm. He was examining the volatile dust, dark green in colour, of *mambe*. Toasted coca leaves, mixed with cecropia wood ash, must be worked in the cylinder until a very fine powder is produced.

After a while Benjamín, the *maloquero*, offers us a container they've filled with the freshly made *mambe*, and a flat little spoon. You have to put a couple of spoonfuls into your mouth and try to form a putty with saliva, initially without swallowing or much less breathing the powder. This putty is pressed into the inside of your cheek and left there. You feel your tongue and lips getting anaesthetized. Gradually a sort of strange lucidity comes over you that activates the desire to talk. It produces a feeling of well-being, and at the same time as embittering your tongue, it loosens it.

The *mambe* brought out of me, perhaps, my uppermost obsessions, the essence of what I am, or aspire to be: a rationalist who believes in Aristotelian logic and in the ideals of the European Enlightenment: universal education, the scientific method, critical scepticism, the democratic system . . . *Mambe*, like all drugs that alter our behaviour, exacerbates qualities or defects: affectionate people become mawkish; anger turns to fury. The rationalist in me became, at least momentarily, a fanatic of science and progress.

I began to argue with Martín von Hildebrand almost impatiently, under the effect of the coca. I told him that just as I had broken with my *Antioqueña*, religious, conservative, Catholic tradition, the Indians also had reasons to doubt their cultural and religious traditions. 'If we've won the permission to attack the God of the Catholics, Muhammad or the God of the Jews, why can I not also attack the indigenous traditions that seem irrational to me?' I asked him. I denied their medicine did any good; I bet their life expectancy was low; I dared him to look at the children's teeth (full of cavities) and toothless gums of the older men; I spoke, rather hot-headedly, of parasites, antibiotics, science and drinking water. I claimed their gods were as false as our saints and medieval gods. And finally, when I was accused of being paternalistic and arrogant, I told him that rationality and logic were not the patrimony of the West but a universal human attribute, in which every culture could participate and in fact does participate. When an Indian chooses a tree to make into a canoe, he is not working from magic thoughts, but choosing the best wood that he knows from experience will make the best craft.

Martín was patient and began to argue within the parameters of my own way of thinking: he told me that if they constructed an aqueduct in the Western way, as I proposed, with pipes carrying safe drinking water to all the houses, and if they installed a power plant to generate electricity, the town would grow even more, and would become unsustainable in this place; increasing the density of the population here would achieve only one thing and that was more conflict over food. I could not impose my world view in the jungle with typical Western arrogance. One of our indigenous guides, Ernesto Ávila – looking slightly worried – was translating bits of our argument for Benjamín and others, and I asked him what he thought. He said he wasn't sure, that he would have to think about it. Edward, with phlegmatic English decorum, kept politely and pensively silent.

We arrived back in San Miguel as night was falling. In the longhouse they had been organizing a gathering, with dances, songs, tales of the past (an odd-sounding stream that resembled the reiterative chants of Tibetan monks) that the orators repeat at full speed while the children and young people listen attentively, looking fascinated. There was also food for everyone, which the women offered us in brimming platters made of hollowed-out gourds. It was during that fiesta that I received the snuff powder, blown up my nose by Yebá-Boso, and perhaps the curse of my future illness. At dawn the next day, when we were meant to embark upriver towards Sónaña, my stomach cramped and diarrhoea sent me running through the village several times.

Physiological Necessities

In the morning, after breakfast, on healthy days, the intestines begin to rumble and call for liberty. In the community of San Miguel, in the middle of the Pirá Paraná austral hemisphere, the custom is the following: beside the hut on stilts where we sleep there is a square-edged shovel stuck in the ground. So you throw the shovel over your shoulder, or, at my age, use it as a walking stick, and cross the small settlement. As you pass you greet children and women, at their domestic chores, and busy men walking here and there. The shovel in your hands reveals clearly where you're going or coming from. They return your greeting or don't, depending on their dispositions.

After leaving behind the village's last house, you arrive at an area of level ground with shrubs. It is a silent, calm place. It does not smell. We all have to do the same thing ('cat style', my instructor in these matters told me): dig a hole in the ground, which is soft and sandy, luckily. Put the excavated earth to one side. The crouched position facilitates and favours the age-old act. It's best not to spend any longer than necessary, for the momentary smell immediately attracts a cloud of various jungle insects. You clean yourself with paper, if available. Then you fill in the hole and replace the earth, making sure everything's well covered. With the shovel over your shoulder and face more relaxed, you stroll back into the settlement.

The morning of our departure I had to make several visits to the piece of ground that served as the toilet area. But finally, towards midday, with my belly on the mend, we embarked. We had ordered several gallons of gasoline, which arrived on another flight from Mitú that came to pick up the Gaia Foundation instructors, so we went upriver in canoes with outboard motors. The journey along this rainforest highway is magnificent. The immense jungle leans over the slow, black, sinuous river. There are enormous trees, of many very different types, some in flower, white-sand beaches, branches that reach out across the river, colourful birds flying over the water, the odd canoe with people fishing patiently close to the shore. The difficult part is getting past the rapids that appear along the river's course. Some can be paddled, lifting the motor's propeller out of the water. Others are unnavigable, so we have to disembark and walk a distance through the jungle, until we get above them. With rucksacks and the motor on our backs, these hikes take us past gigantic trees, stinking swamps, crystal-clear waterfalls.

Sónaña

We reach Sónaña at dusk. The river gets darker by the minute, quieter, almost gloomy. The part of the settlement that's near the river, however, is nice. There is a boarding school with children from various communities, and indigenous teachers. A wooden chapel, both simple and dignified. But we will be sleeping in a *maloca* a few kilometres inland. The old *maloquero* there is Chico, though his son, Faustino, is domineering. Faustino had travelled along the river separately from us and arrived slightly earlier. I notice that neither Faustino nor his relatives welcome us enthusiastically; there is no joy among those who take us in. Maybe they already know we're arriving without food and they obviously have none to spare.

When Faustino speaks, with his rancid *mambe* breath (both cheeks enlarged, the remains of two greenish teeth), there is something harsh in his voice. Resentful protests. A ferocious grimace. His way of speaking is complaining and violent. I offer him unfiltered cigarettes and some pesos to thank him for the hospitality, and he doesn't just accept them but snatches them out of my hands, voraciously and fast like a piranha.

At night he talks of killing those who approach his lands with malevolent intentions. He speaks well of himself, of his profound knowledge of traditions, and badly of other Indians, who he says are lazy thieves. He makes an issue of the gasoline, which he believes to be his to distribute as he sees fit; he seems jealous and suspicious of Reynel, who will be our next host in Puerto Ortega.

I spend a very bad night in Chico's *maloca*. The longhouse is invaded by rats with and without wings, lizards, cockroaches and mosquitoes. The smoke from the fire sets off my asthma. I open my compass and notice that the north and south doors are not precisely aligned to their cardinal points, as they should be. Everything here appears to have been constructed lethargically, carelessly. I have nightmares with horrible visions of death and violence, in which Faustino and his father put me on trial as an ally of the Western World and condemn me to be burned at the stake. When I wake up I feel trapped there, in danger. It seems like the slightest argument would be enough for them to attack us. I hear the tale of an indigenous man who, according to them, poisoned a woman with game, and she died shortly after eating it. When they buried her they threw water over the corpse, and the thread of water pointed to the hunter who had given her the meat. This was more than sufficient demonstration of his guilt. They had to organize an expedition of men to take revenge. They beat him and his entire family to death, so not a trace of his wickedness would remain on the earth. The verdict of the gods had been given by the thread of water that pointed towards him. No one says who killed him and his family, so they won't get into trouble with the white man's justice system. This is an ancient form of ancestral justice, which is best not discussed in public. The poisoner got his just deserts, and that's all there is to it.

I only surface from my apprehensions and bad feelings halfway through the morning, with the sunlight and a cool waterfall. I go for a swim with Edward (educated, serene and reflective), and we share thoughts and experiences. The fresh water and frank conversation in English about what we've seen dispel my anxiety. It's a new day and I relax when I find out that Martín has decided we'll carry on upriver today, and not sleep another night in Sónaña, as I had feared. When I ask Faustino for a shovel before my usual morning necessities, he tells me rudely that they don't use shovels there, that I should just go find some place in the woods to defecate.

Puerto Ortega

As soon as we leave Sónaña, to travel further up the Pirá Paraná River, the mood improves. There is not only warmth and smiles, but also that unquestionable sign of intelligence: curiosity. They are interested in my watch with its compass and altimeter; they enquire about my metal hip flask of whisky (which I give to Edward and Martín, because I can't drink any alcohol, with my stomach in a bad way).

Puerto Ortega is the smallest of all the communities we visit. It has, says Martín, suitable dimensions for the rainforest. We are greeted by Reynel's elderly father in the *maloca*, and in another house by Reynel's wife and their daughters, who welcome us with pineapples, bananas, cassava and a delicious spicy soup of boiled fish. I eat well for the first time since I arrived in the jungle, and in a friendly, cheerful atmosphere. The settlement's site has been well chosen: at the river's edge there is a soft, white sandy beach and the cold, not too turbulent water is a delight. Small children jump into the current in groups and swim strongly across the river and back again; the current carries them downstream and they arrive at the other side much further down, but they have it all calculated. They also paddle across, without the slightest difficulty. I, who am supposedly a strong swimmer, do not dare try to cross it, out of fear that the current will sweep me over the nearby rapids; the children, however, swim and paddle across over and over again, joyfully, back and forth. I see that here too they take a shovel into the woods and with my compass I observe that the *maloca* doors are perfectly aligned to the north and south. These elemental details of mental order and hygiene are undoubtedly steps forward on the path of a word anthropologists hate: progress. The dogs of Puerto Ortega, furthermore, are not starving, as they were in

Sónaña (and in parts of San Miguel), but healthy, and they are well treated, for thanks to them the hunting is better: they are mankind's long-standing allies, and even bark every once in a while, when they see us go past. The ones in Sónaña couldn't spare the energy.

Reynel has a small son who sticks to him like a tic, with almost desperate affection and devotion. His father treats him tenderly, hugs him, strokes him, picks parasites out of his hair and crushes the nits between his fingernails, and they die there with a tiny final explosion. The boy is chubby, healthy and alert. The women treat him with affection too, and also cook the best cassava I've tasted in any of the river communities. It's crispy on the outside and soft within, a bit like French sourdough bread. Reynel's wife, with a hard swat, saves me from a horsefly bite. Suddenly I feel safe, and well, even protected by others.

Hunting

Our guide Adán invites us to go hunting with him. We leave quite late, after nine: Adán, Edward, a paddler and me. The moon will be bright, and that's bad for hunting, but it's not up yet or is still hidden behind the clouds. We get a canoe from the stream that feeds into the river, pushing out into the current, by the light of our torches. When we turn them off, absolutely nothing can be seen. We drift downriver, only using the paddles to steer the canoe. Adán requests silence with a gesture and his flashlight beam inspects the shores. He's searching for the eyes of an agouti. In the dark night only the eyes of animals reflect light, like two still and symmetrical diamonds, like two perfectly aligned fireflies. The beam of my flashlight sweeps across the surface of the water, skilfully controlled by Adán. When he points it at the treetops they seem to move threateningly. We drift downriver for a long time, without seeing any animals; when the moon comes out everything takes on an extraordinary silvery tone, bad for hunting but fantastic for the nocturnal outing on the water. In the distance, we begin to hear the rapids, the current lashing against the sharp rocks.

My heart starts to race; if we got caught in the current, the canoe would be smashed to pieces against the rocks, and us along with it. It's time to go back upriver, says Adán. They decide to turn on the outboard motor. Adán keeps scanning the banks with the flashlight beam. Suddenly he makes a very slow gesture with one hand and asks us to approach the bank. The beam shines directly on a pair of brilliant dots; the animal's eyes do not blink, as if paralysed. Adán hesitates for a moment; picks up the rifle and almost immediately puts it back down again in the bow. Shots are very expensive in Amazonia (the Army puts heavy restrictions on the sale of bullets and cartridges, for fear they'll fall into the guerrillas' hands), and they save them whenever they can. Adán grabs one of the paddles, leaps onto land like a tiger and begins to bludgeon an animal we can't see. He attacks furiously, without a word or a sound. A short while later he returns with a caiman over his shoulder; blood drips into the water from its small head. He throws it disdainfully into the bottom of the boat. We carry on upriver, paddling now, with the motor off. The caiman revives all of a sudden and begins to thrash desperately up and down the length of the canoe. Edward and I emit the clumsy hysterical yelps of civilized men and lift our bare feet in fear of a bite. Adán laughs, grabs his paddle by one end and gives the poor caiman one last definitive blow.

It's the only result of our night's hunt and will be our breakfast the next day. Caiman meat is white and very tasty, but I barely touch it, with certain distant and absurd qualms. If I lived in the jungle with this intermittent vegetarian fussiness, I'd starve to death. After breakfast Edward and I go with Adán to swim in the river, and to fish. It is at least thirty degrees Celsius in the shade; the water, however, is twenty-five degrees and it's a pleasure to swim against the current. We paddle upstream until we get tired, then let the canoe drift downstream and Adán starts casting his line with great precision, towards the river's edge. The fish aren't biting. The river water is very acidic, and there aren't many big fish. Another canoe passes us full of ice-cream bean pods. They give us a pile of these, sweet and refreshing, delicious fruits. Seeing we haven't caught any fish, they also give us a small catfish 'so you won't go home empty-handed', they say, laughing. Finally a tiny white fish bites Adán's hook. That was the result of a night's hunting and a morning's fishing: one caiman and one little fish – not enough to feed a family.

On our last night in Puerto Ortega we all sit around the fire talking, around the age-old hearth.

To keep from getting sleepy, the men have a constant supply of *mambe*, and every once in a while they sniff tobacco blown directly into each other's nostrils. I was one of the first to retire from the masculine circle of conversation each night, and this last night in Puerto Ortega as well. Nevertheless, lying in my hammock, with my blurry myopic vision, I carried on listening to that almost ritual conversation for a while, until the very syllables would start to put me to sleep.

Reflections at the End of the Trip

I arrived back from the jungle, as I said at the beginning, very ill and with a rare paralysis of willpower. Writing these memories has cost me weeks of introspection and many doubts. I'm still not even in agreement with myself. In the jungle many things mislead us. My own illness completely misled the Western doctors who treated me in Medellín. Because I'd come from there I consulted experts in tropical medicine; they ruled out malaria, dengue fever, other parasites. As always when they don't know what a person has, they concluded that it must be a very aggressive virus and recommended liquids and rest. The fever and discomfort continued. Finally my internal medicine specialist found the trouble, looking at new tests and X-rays: pneumonia was slowly and dangerously taking over my lungs. I didn't submit to prayers or diets, but rather to a course of antibiotics, and gradually got better. I believe my fate would have been harsher, and with worse results, in the jungle. I also believe, superstitiously, that the hex did come from Yebá-Boso's mouth and breath, though I don't think he meant to transmit a bacterium from his lungs into mine. It simply happened. It happened and I got over it and we both survived; he with his rites and I with my Western medicine. In this magnificent country called Colombia, we coexist with Indians living as they have for thousands of years and their acculturated descendants, and the acculturated descendants of Africans and Europeans, like those of us who live in the cities of the Andes. We have centuries ahead of us, and our descendants can live through them together, side by side, if we coexist by respecting and mixing their culture with ours. Instead of isolating ourselves, we should exchange ideas and choose the best of what there is within and outside of the jungle. ■

TOUR GUIDE

Phil Klay

'Join the Army! Travel to exotic, distant lands, meet exciting, unusual people, and then kill them.' It's an old joke that's only half joking. It's no accident that Western culture's first bit of travel writing is *The Odyssey*. Travel and war go together by necessity. My time in service led me to Germany, Kuwait and Iraq. I've got friends who, courtesy of the Marine Corps, saw Kenya, the Mediterranean, Thailand, Australia and Serbia. The promise of travel, at least, proved true. I never even saw combat, but I did go to Baghdad and see the much-photographed Swords of Qādisīyah. I didn't take any pictures there, though. I still had romantic notions of war, and I didn't want to come back to America with any photos that would let my friends and family mistake my deployment for tourism.

How strange, then, to see the end of World War II through Colonel Claude A. Black's lens. Colonel Black was a staff officer in the 9th Army, one of the main combat commands in the European theatre, but the photos in his album start off looking like tourist snaps, with typical tourist annotations ('One-time palace of German Emperors. Fine murals depicting legendary history of Germany' or 'A German shepherd – working his flock on autobahn'). The album becomes increasingly bizarre as it follows him across France and Germany. Prettily framed shots of Cornwall and Cannes sit uneasily alongside pages titled 'Picturesque Germany', and then, perversely, 'Slave Labour Germany'. These photos, and the photos of buildings turned to rubble and destroyed war materiel, stand eloquently devoid of comment.

Perhaps no comment was necessary. I can easily imagine Colonel Black wanting to remember which precise location it was that boasted those fine murals of Germany's legendary history. Noting those details down is only common sense. I have a harder time imagining him forgetting the day he saw his first Nazi guard tower.

Who's the person behind all these images? What did he think, going from Cannes to fields of burned-out panzers? But what he thought, we won't ever know. We don't have access to Colonel Black's reactions, only our own.

I take photos for much the same reason I underline and make notes in the margins of the books I read: not because I intend to go back and look at all but a few of those notes ever again, but because the act of recording itself is part of the experience. I read a passage and I'm moved, but that emotion is not enough, be it pleasure, horror or joy. Emotions demand a physical response. To anchor that sentiment requires a physical mark: a thinly traced line, an illegibly scrawled note, a photograph.

Errol Morris says that photos 'provide a "window" into history. Not into general history – but into a specific moment, a specific place. It is as if we have reached into the past and created a tiny peephole.' Photographs are a small purchase on some kind of truth separate from the lies we tell ourselves through memory and the lies we tell our families through letters and emails home. 'Here is the irrefutable reality,' the photos say. 'I was here. I looked through the viewfinder, saw this scene and recorded it.' It's the very strength of that claim that causes problems. With so much assurance about what's inside the frame, why should we bother wondering what's left out?

My favourite images from my own deployment paint a false portrait of the year I spent mostly at a desk, earning combat pay. Photo: me in an Iraqi town, carrying an M4 I borrowed from HQ Company. Photo: me in a convoy. Me in a meeting with Iraqi police. Me looking tough with my marines.

I'm hardly the only one to practise selective wartime photography. Recently I shared a few beers with a three-time Purple Heart recipient. 'The first time I got shot it fucking sucked,' he told me, which wasn't much of a revelation in and of itself, but when I asked him why, his answer was more interesting.

'I was so tired and all I wanted to do was go to sleep,' he said. But he couldn't – word had spread that a marine had been injured and soon friends and acquaintances and even a good number of marines he didn't get along with all dropped by with a specific purpose in mind. 'Everybody in my unit,' he said, 'wanted have their picture taken with me.'

So much is left out of the frame. Travel photography tends to forgo documentation of plane rides, customs, wrong turns in unfamiliar streets, in favour of the Taj Mahal, the Eiffel Tower, the friend shot impressively-but-not-too-seriously in the face. We record the reality we're *supposed* to have, and then go back later and tell ourselves that it was the reality we experienced.

This is why I didn't want a photograph of myself at the Swords of Qādisīyah. Such a photo would be out-and-out tourism, like Colonel Black's shots of Cannes. To be a tourist implies a detachment from the world the tourist is immersed in, whereas war is a place of life-and-death decisions with no room for detachment. Or so I thought.

Perhaps that's what seems wrong with Colonel Black's album. World War II is supposed to be more adventure, more horror and less Picturesque Germany. It's not the mix I wanted for my war photography, but maybe Colonel Black was a more honest photographer than I was. We'll never know. We can't see what he didn't show us. ∎

TOUR GUIDE

From the
Archive of Modern Conflict

① Dec 1944
Maastricht Holland
a candid Made one
night at office
Armored Section
by Cpt Zipping—
Note Blackout
curtain or screen in
place on window.
Also note cantern
on shelf.

② Gattersloe, Germany, April 1945 – Watching a
demonstration of First Recoilless Rifles we had.
Sgt Frank Rider took this picture as a candid.
Note that the old man (Col Gen Simpson) looks mad.
He was some ? old ? mad ? enraged the
demonstration. First place this area was not
marked so was hard to find. Rider, Oldham & I
looked 20 minutes or so south of the Autobahn
from Ninth Army. Finally found it by talking
to men. Later they had had trouble trouble started
fires of old grenade Note Rack also Jeep in
some treatment today but the old Jeep is
fire close here is blanket ? ? Sgt screen ?

Bristol, England 1944

③ Muir House "X" is
window of Room Ralph
Tibbets & I had.

④ Garden and
Rose Tree
Muir House

⑤ Part of Clifton College
Buildings

⑥ Supply Room HQ Ninth Army

⑦ Cricket Field Foreground
Main Buildings, Clifton College
Bristol, England

⑧ Entrance Gate to
field & college shown
in ⑦

Cornwall, England 1944

(9)

(10)

(11)

(12)

(13)

(14)

(15)

Most beautiful spot in Normandy - Near Pre'en Pal

(16) Curate's House   (17) Henri Fouquex   (18) Church - Madame Georges Rousset

Saw this place first in August 1944 when following 3rd A.D. to Falaise Gap. Remembered and revisited in July 1945 while waiting at Deauville for boot to U.S.A. Made above pictures

(19) Cathedral where William the conqueror had mass said before invading England   (20) wreck of cathedral at Caen where British invaded June 1944 (21)

(22) Normandy Hotel (23) and Beach "....." (24) at Deauville France where HqNinth Army stayed July 1945

Cannes France June 1945
(9 day Rest + recouperation - a "restee" 25 June - 4 July)

25)   "La Croisette"
26)
27) View from window in my room in Hotel Ptr de Esquillion in distance

28) Yacht Basin + swimming place Isle de St. Honorat
29) Return from day of sailing - Girl in center is Mary Ryan of "Top Hat" famp. other girl Eldie Shriver from California I believe. I was wet + cold.
30)

31) Juan, — Mary Ryan in front of Gate of New Capuchin Monistary
32) "Pedalos"
33) Well in center of mother monistary of Capuchin Order

Eden Rock – Juan les Pins
See map pasted in back

(34) (35) (36)

Water cold, blue and rough – Ran into
"Baron" Kem here.

(37) viewing the   (38) Monte Carlo   (39) Roman Monument
beauties of nature   on Roman Road Near
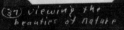   Italian Border.

(40)   (41)
Mount Blanc Switzerland from a   C-47   July 4 1945

(42) X My office in
the Caserne Oct 1944
March 1945 - these windows
shattered by bomb midnight 31 Dec

(43) Signal Center
Hq Ninth
Army

(44) Bridge Between
Caserne + Our
Quarters - Picture does
Not do it Justice

(45) Main Square +
Cathedral
Maastricht

(46) Hotel du Casque
Jack Spragur + I
Occupied Room Shown

(47) Sunday Morning
July 1945
Murphy Thompson +
Russ Smith - Step out
on way from Brunswick
to Deauville

(48)   (49)   (50)
Old wall and Gate

Limberg Province Holland 1945

(60)

(61)

(62)

(63)

(64) Grotto near
Volken berg Holland

(74) One-time palace of German Emperors. Fine Murals depicting legendary History of Germany. Goslar

(75) Some of Best examples of Medieval Architecture Extant. Goslar — 50 miles south Brunswick in Hartz Mountains.

(76)

(77) C. P. of 747 Th B4 Quedlinburg G. June 1945

(78) Typical Farm Compound Near Magdeburg

(79) Autobahn near Gottingen

(80) Iron work- Brunswick

(81)

(82) Autobahn Near Brunswick

(83) A German Shepherd - working his flock on Autobahn
between Brunswick + Magdeburg. One dog keeps flock
out of rye field, another keeps sheep out of road
a third relief dog leashed to shepherds belt.

(84)

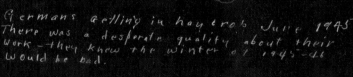

(85)

Germans getting in hay crop June 1945
There was a desperate quality about their
work — they knew the winter of 1945-46
would be bad.

Slave Labor Germany

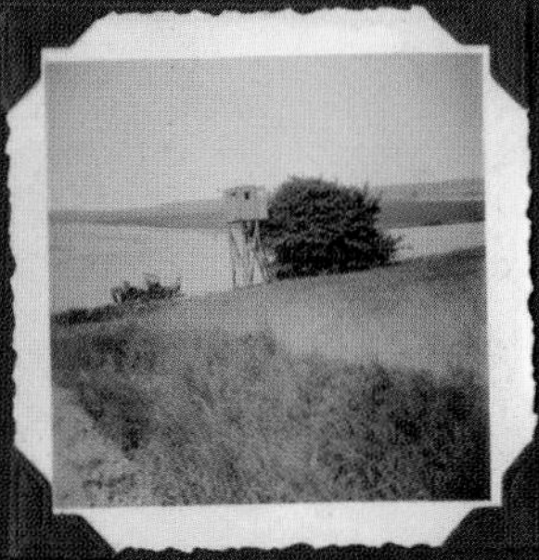

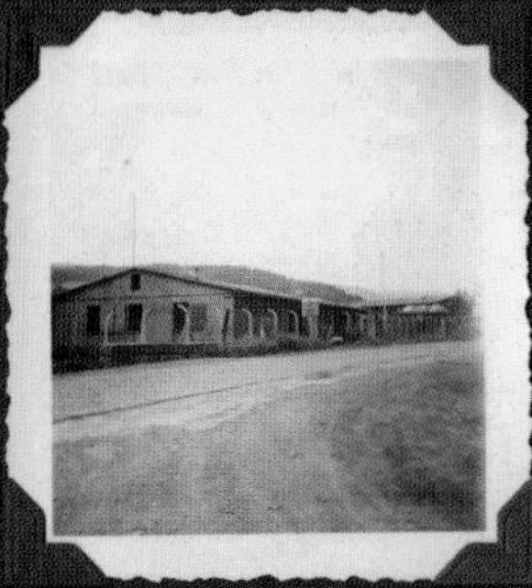

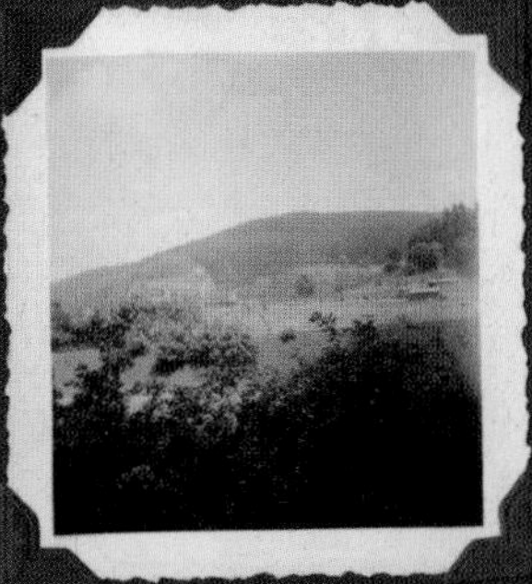

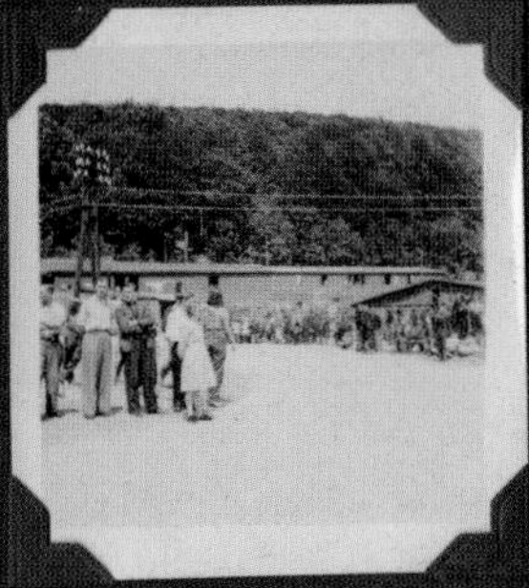

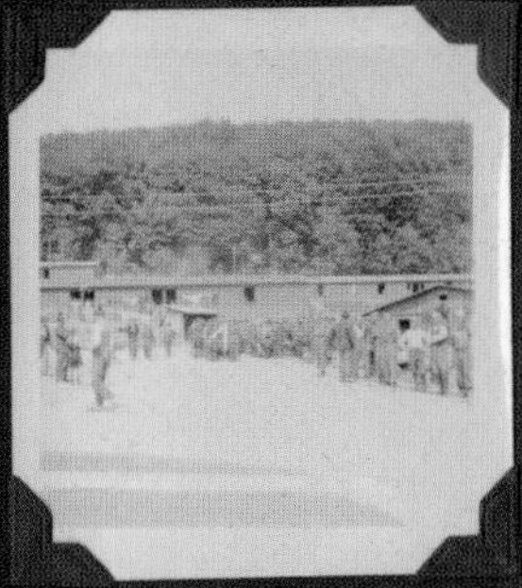

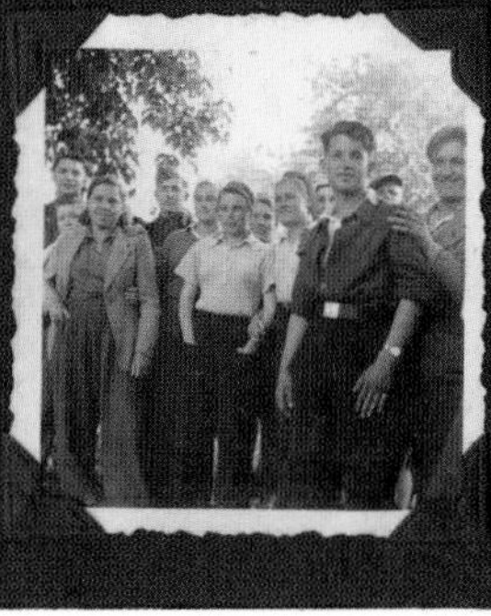

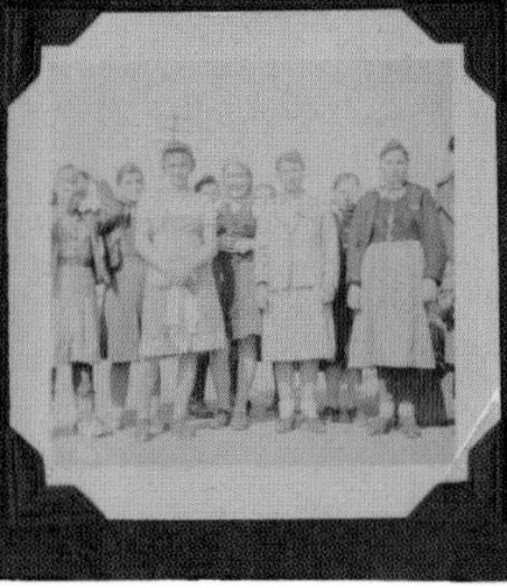

BARRENLAND

A Yi

TRANSLATED FROM THE CHINESE BY ERIC ABRAHAMSEN

After one year and seven months in Hongyi country, I finally left it behind for good. As the rattle-trap jeep reached proper asphalt I felt the light dawn on my face: nine months before the end of the century and I was at last escaping from that pit, that man-trap of a place. My father would stand in the doorway of our home in the county capital to welcome me and I would never tell him all the things I'd done in that place, or the fact that I almost didn't make it home.

My last item of official business in Hongyi was going to see a corpse. I'd stopped caring about work by that point. I turned away the people who trudged a few – or a few dozen – kilometres to the police station for an ID card or their housing registration, citing some minor omission in their preparations. 'Come try again in a few days,' I said with a smile. In a few days I'd be gone forever. I winked at the unregistered motorcycle that barrelled down the road, piloted with great arrogance by an attractive young man with sideburns, an equally attractive girl grasping his waist and leaning her head against his leather jacket, eyes closed in obvious pleasure. I hated to disturb them, though they were clearly trying to provoke me by zooming back and forth in front of the police station.

The corpse I went to see was lying beside a paddy far from any village, a place unfrequented since the autumn harvest. First the frost had fallen on the rice stubble, then snow had covered everything over. It was a dog that found the body. It had barked at the corpse all morning before its owner finally went after it with a stick. The station chief and I walked there together, the snow under our feet like soft, waterlogged wood. The chief was saying, 'You've got to think things through carefully.' I assumed he was cautioning me not to hurt a certain girl I was seeing; or possibly he was exhorting me not to ruin myself for her sake. At any rate, I was meant to make the responsible choice. He started talking about how he met his wife. We all knew she'd originally been a rural resident, now unemployed, and had a terrible temper. He said how good their life was now, thanks to love. I knew it was bullshit. 'If you're going to be with her, then be with her,' he said. 'Otherwise, break it off now.'

The corpse was less than 1.5 metres tall, laid out rigid and tidy as a Popsicle along a gradually inclining road. The snowmelt had turned its hair to a particularly intense black. It was clothed in a tattered quilted jacket with multicoloured patches and old black cotton trousers. The face and palms displayed livid purple spots – as the coroner explained, the spots would disappear on a living person if you pressed on them, but once you released the pressure and the blood resumed its flow, the spots reappeared. You can imagine how, after death, gravity draws a corpse's blood into its lowermost veins. We heaved the stiff corpse up and over, and it thumped heavily to the ground. A tranquil face, with fine hairs at the corners of the mouth, revealing neither suffering nor repose, masculinity nor femininity. The chief squatted down and undid the cloth belt around the trousers, pulling them down. There was a deep bruised depression in the exposed waist, and I saw a stone protruding from the ground where the corpse had been lying. The deceased had fallen upon the stone at the moment of death. The chief stopped with the trousers partway down: 'It's a woman,' he said. 'She's got stretch marks.' I didn't look. The dog came bounding back, prancing like a child. The chief said to its owner, 'Leash it.'

We judged, from her possessions, that she was a beggar, perhaps retarded or mentally disturbed, but at least aware of the Spring Festival. In this snow-swept season she'd been attempting to return to the place of her birth; this little road led to the neighbouring province, a distance of four or five, perhaps a dozen, kilometres. Who knew where she'd come from, how long she'd been walking before she collapsed on the road? In the village where she belonged, perhaps the lamps were already lit.

It was the only actual corpse I ever saw in Hongyi, though there was one other death. On that occasion, when I arrived at the scene on my motorcycle all I saw was a round pit in the bridge, the size of a bowl, the consequence of a mighty strike from the fist of God, though it hadn't penetrated the steel-reinforced concrete of the bridge. Torrential rains created a mad wash of water under it, as though the waves themselves were fighting to stay afloat. I never saw the bicycle, but they said it had been smashed out of shape, as if it had been run over by a truck. The deceased, named Gong Jin, had been a bricklayer, and I still remember the way he always leaped hurriedly onto his bicycle, left foot pedalling and right kicking off the ground to get up to speed. Then he would arch his back, both legs pedalling furiously, his buttocks raised off the seat.

The day he died, black clouds had gathered in the sky, and the rain came suddenly. 'Why are you in such a hurry to get back?' teased a female passer-by.

Gong Jin only chuckled.

He was a jolly fellow. When he understood it was about to rain a sudden look of realization had come over his face, as if he'd left something outside that mustn't get wet. Before the lightning began, the clouds converged like two great black tanks rumbling and booming. My colleague Wang, bare-chested, headed for Shuanggang River carrying a bucketful of dirty laundry, Lux soap and Head & Shoulders shampoo. He washed in the river all year round, in winter first squatting at the edge and splashing himself to get used to the cold. We were all in the habit of putting the shampoo directly on our dry hair, then pouring on a little water and slowly working up a lather – not like other bathers, who always dunked themselves first. It was part of our style. Country people and city people are different. 'You're washing now? Aren't you afraid you'll be electrocuted?' I asked.

Wang didn't even turn his head. 'When your time's up, you're tits up.'

The thunder was furious, ringing over the hills like vast cymbals, with a metallic reverberation. An instant of profound darkness followed a sudden extinguishing, followed instantly by a claw of light. Gong Jin, who'd been pushing his bike over the bridge at a run, was dead. The lightning was deadly accurate. From that day on I thought of God as the Cheka agent that Mandelstam saw at the feast, obviously drunk on vodka, placing a stack of blank forms on the table, casually condemning people to arrest or execution as he filled them out. Gong Jin's death left me clinging tightly to that girl in bed, and swearing, like anyone who's been overcome by the absurd, that I would take care of her, that I wouldn't let God snatch her away, that the two of us would live in peace, and on and on in that vein. Later I would bitterly regret saying all that.

I had arrived in Hongyi in September of 1997, at dusk. Two months before that I'd left the provincial capital for Ruichang county (the State Council had elevated it to a municipality in 1989, but with only 400,000 residents it was still just a county to us), passing through Jiujiang on the way. When I'd dragged my luggage through the gate of the provincial capital's Public Security Vocational Training School, the guard at the gate, in a white undershirt, roused himself from the languor of the permanent city resident and called to his brainless son. The latter ran out, rolling his eyes and giggling, to close and latch the gate behind me. The city's sturdy skyscrapers and its proliferating, endlessly twirling neon lights winked out like fragments of a dream. Even that idiot's fate seemed preferable to mine. And now the Ruichang County Public Security Bureau had assigned me to a patch of countryside I'd never even heard of, sixty-seven kilometres to the north-west, at the edge of Jiangxi province. 'It's big,' my father said confidently, after a moment of earnest thought. 'A lot of people.' It took a whole afternoon in the police jeep to get there. Every time we pulled over at some little market town I thought we'd arrived, but we were just repairing the jeep. That jeep gulped down petrol like an alcoholic, collapsing afterwards at the side of the road.

The cumulative repair fees had long ago exceeded the price of a replacement, but the police station never managed to scrape the full amount together at once.

The driver was taciturn, and sported a red birthmark on his forehead. He'd got this menial job through an introduction from his brother-in-law, an officer who, while working at the police station, had become involved with a dressmaker next door. She was the driver's elder sister; her registration was rural, and so was his. Behind the eyes of those with rural registrations lies a deep anxiety, inferiority, awe, even guilt. They stand before those with urban registrations as the blacks must have once stood before the whites in America. It was only recently, at the age of thirty-six, that I realized the reason I could never express my feelings to the first girl I loved wasn't because I feared something in her character or personality, but because I suspected she knew about my prior legal status. Before being accepted at university my registration was rural – the son of a peasant woman in a county-level town. You rarely hear of city girls marrying the sons of peasant women, though some men in the city do marry country girls, perhaps to ease the loneliness.

We pulled onto Hongyi Street in silence. There wasn't an inch of real asphalt in the place, which I'd been led to believe was flourishing. Trucks passing after rainfall had raised great ruts in the road, and the places that seemed level were simply filled in with gravel, perfect for puncturing bicycle tyres. The whole street was less than a hundred metres long, dotted with places like a credit union, grain station and land-use office along with stores selling vegetables, meat and articles of daily use. There was a postal agency run by a rural household, a petrol station stocked with buckets of petrol (the proprietor refuelled vehicles by sucking on a rubber hose to get the flow started before sticking it in the gas tank), a hair salon, a pool table with ruined felt and a little restaurant converted from a residential dwelling (it had no sign, nor did it need one). The police station was originally located above this restaurant, and only later moved to the credit union's old building. That was it for the street: only a few steps long, the urban centre of a rural administration zone 100.5 square kilometres in area, a place rural residents might spend their entire lives trying to squeeze into. To me, however, it was the gully into which the train of my life had plunged after jumping its rails. It was after 9 p.m., and the street was pitch black and deserted. After retiring to the small room that had been allotted to me, I couldn't be bothered unpacking, instead flopping into a chair like a frog and blanking out. The sound of the rushing river came from the distance. The next day they would boast repeatedly to me of this fifteen-kilometre-long, westward-running river – all the rest of the world's rivers ran east, they said. I guess it was a sort of dull humour.

I never encountered a single criminal case in Hongyi. No rape, no robbery, no murder. It seemed that our only real duty was to keep up appearances by ensuring there was meat on the table. During the daytime we were idle, reading the newspaper in the morning sunlight, a cup of hot water to hand, disturbed only by a visitor or two who needed something done. At ten or eleven at night we'd pile into the jeep and visit some nearby village. We'd stop a kilometre or so before we arrived and get out to walk the rest of the way – we reminded each other not to wear leather shoes, because they made our footsteps audible. Nearly everyone was already in bed with the lights out, but mah-jong games could be going on in the still-lit houses. We'd creep up to the door and listen to what was going on – if money was trading hands we'd burst inside. We were like hunters, waiting for the right instant to pounce. A moment too late or too soon and we might lose our prey: they could always say they were just playing for fun, not gambling. We'd usually take the prey back with us and fine them; we'd get a certain proportion of the take back from the finance department, and that counted as our income. We were always short of operating funds: petrol and repairs for the vehicles, salaries for the driver and militiamen, money for food supplies – we even had to scrimp for our own salaries. Often we returned empty-handed. The jeep carried us out brimming with hope, and carried us back washed in despair. All that wasted petrol . . . We were like poor fishermen who'd not only failed to land a catch, but also lost the net we'd bought with our last bit of cash.

On 13 January 1998, fifteen days before the Chinese New Year, a fellow officer, a militiaman, and I were ordered to take the jeep to a village called Donghang, all for the sake of a mere four hundred yuan. It was on a hilltop, five hundred metres or more above sea level, a drive of a dozen kilometres or so. We stopped at a mountain ridge and got out to walk a two-kilometre trail, after which the four of us (including the driver) easily apprehended a gambler who'd returned home for the holidays. He was named Cheng Qian, and we'd once broken up a mah-jong game he'd been playing in. He had fled, but we'd caught the other three and fined them four hundred yuan each – you could say we were going to collect a debt. At a juncture in the winding path, Cheng Qian took advantage of the rain-wet earth to give us the slip. In a moment he was several dozen metres away while we still stood there, open-mouthed and blinking, as though watching a fish slip from our hands into the water. 'Stop or I'll shoot!' I shouted. He stopped and slowly turned round – by then he was too far away to see clearly, but he appeared to be trembling in terror. But as soon as he could see that I held up nothing but my finger, of course he kept running.

On 23 August 2010, while attempting to rescue twenty-two Hong Kong tourists from the bus in which they were being held hostage, a Filipino police officer had also brandished his finger, a photograph that was seen around the world. I think there's something profoundly ridiculous about a police officer who has not been issued a gun. In 1922, while acting as a police officer in Myanmar, Eric Blair clumsily shot an elephant that had previously been on a rampage, all to avoid appearing foolish before a crowd of some 2,000 locals who had gathered to watch. In order to avoid losing face in front of the 170,000 inhabitants of Hongyi, we went to our jeep to get our flashlights, and returned to Donghang. Cheng Qian was long gone. Then, in our anger and frustration, we made a very stupid mistake:

we tried to cart off his Sichuanese girlfriend, who'd come home with him for the holidays.

We imagined that once we had her at the station, Cheng Qian would turn himself in. A straight trade: him in exchange for her; a man in exchange for his woman. We imagined carting off the woman would be a simple matter. Instead we found ourselves tugging on an obstinate vine that attached itself to every object in the house. She collapsed to the floor to maximize friction and her feet seemed to hook like anchors on everything they touched. In order to speed the process along we whacked her with our flashlights, and she began performing an on-the-verge-of-death act: frothing at the mouth, ranting and occasionally wheezing as though she were taking her last breaths. We started to realize what a mess we were in, but it was too late to stop. Everyone in the village surrounded us, holding clubs, poles and machetes – even brooms. One hulking fellow held a 'brush spear', a tool for carrying firewood that consisted of a thick, heavy pole, the ends of which tapered into half-inch-long iron flanges. After the mountain people had cut their wood they would tie it into two bundles, then stick one on each end of the brush spear. It took a lot of strength to drive the point right through the bundles, and the iron flanges, originally black, were scraped clean and bright from use. The man snorted at us through his nose. 'Everyone stay calm!' I kept saying, though my mind was a blank. Finally the elusive Cheng Qian came charging back, waving a cleaver over his head, and said in tones of terrible judgement, 'Why did you beat my woman?' The crowd parted as he approached, and everyone watched open-mouthed as he began to chop at the muscular arm of the militiaman with the cleaver. All of us – police and locals – were rooted to the spot with terror, until suddenly the militiaman snatched the cleaver and took off running at a great clip. Cheng Qian had attacked him with the back of the blade; later he found blood blisters beneath the skin of his arm. I followed the militiaman at a quick walk. My remaining colleagues exchanged a glance and then, like pantomime actors who must remain silent and thus pour all their effort and ingenuity into their limbs, began to sprint, so fast they lofted the mud behind them. The wind of their flight swept over me. After reaching a safe distance the militiaman stopped and waved the cleaver. 'It's over for you, Cheng Qian, the evidence is right here!' The villagers obligingly gave chase, and only then did I realize it was the evidence itself that the honest bunch wanted, not the man who held it. They understood little about the law and thought that the mere existence of the cleaver was enough to establish guilt, meaning jail time and maybe even execution. I continued to walk at a brisk pace, one foot on the ground at all times. For fuck's sake, I was thinking, I'm still in uniform, and someone in uniform shouldn't scamper around like a mouse. The pursuers broke over me like a wave and ran on ahead, and they didn't even see me until they were on their way back. It's hard to describe their change of expression – from extreme dejection, even heartsickness, to the sudden joy of an unexpected windfall. Many pairs of hands grasped my arms and bore me back to the village. Darkness was falling like a well being gradually lidded. I raised my face and silently repeated the name of my very first love. Meimei . . . Meimei. She had never given me a second glance, she was an impenetrable fortress, but she was all I had to lend me strength. I'm going to die, Meimei.

The villagers spent a long time trying to frighten me, and forced me to sign a statement of confession, but even now I think of them as good people. Or perhaps it wasn't goodness, but a mousy terror of getting into trouble. It's why Cheng Qian attacked with the back of his cleaver and not the blade, and why they insisted I sign a statement that our seizure of the Sichuanese woman was unjustified. They just wanted to keep things from passing the point of no return. Later they got in contact with a fellow villager who worked in the provincial government, who then contacted a county-level leader, and the whole business blew over.

M ost of the time, I was at a loss as to how to pass the day. When the weather was warm I'd go to the river, leaning my head on the concrete bank and letting my body soak until it wrinkled. When I couldn't sleep I'd write love letters. I couldn't say for sure if I'd really been in love with Meimei, my old high-school classmate. If she'd been willing I certainly wouldn't have declined, but it didn't matter if she ignored me, if she went on ignoring me forever. I just needed someone I could address myself to in the middle of the night. It was always something grand: *For you, I have gladly placed myself on the altar of love, where I crackle and singe. For you I am ruined, I am sacrificed.* One night, while I was writing something along those lines, a brief melody sounded from the tape player, only three or four seconds in length. It was anguished and plunging, like the moment of utter vertigo as you're being swept over a waterfall. My nose prickled. Just as I prepared to surrender myself to the pleasure of tears, the song ended. The one that followed was far too cheerful, and I scrambled to rewind the tape. First I went too far, and then not far enough – by the time I found that passage again it was still melancholy, but no longer heartbreaking. After the fourth repetition, I realized it was no different from any other melody. To extend my precious melancholic mood, I tried something I'd learned during military training at school: I opened my eyes wide and stared at the light without blinking. Soon afterwards my aching eyes produced a single enormous tear. I quickly picked up the letter to catch it. It fell heavily, like the first drop of a spring shower, but there was only the one. I sealed the letter but never sent it. Everyone like me, young people who'd come from elsewhere to work in the countryside, was feeling bored and empty, and we spent a lot of time chatting and drinking together, discussing life in the distant cities and gossiping about local scandals. We'd get ourselves stinking drunk. At night in the fields behind the station you could hear the sound of puking as we stuck our fingers down our throats, hacking up thick gobs of vomitus that reeked like chemical fertilizer while we howled like wolves.

On one particularly hot night we couldn't find the well bucket, and an inebriated Wang lay down at the lip of the well, lowering himself inside head first until he could scoop up water to drink. It took him ages to inch his way back out. On another night a few of us young men, driven by the storms of passion, found ourselves a disco ball, a boom box and a dance music tape. We took it all to the conference room of the local government building, pushed aside the tables and chairs, and danced. After about a half-hour a local government leader put a stop to it, and we hated him for it. We thought of ourselves as very poor – we had nothing but time, and too much of that. None of us owned anything except our lust. We were like animals, snuffling around with our heads down, in search of the imagined scent of romance.

I had two girlfriends while I was there. In both cases, I warned myself ahead of time: it's a clamp that women have down there – once you put it in you'll never get it out, not as long as you live. I'd learned from the mistakes of others; I'd seen it happen to the brother-in-law of the driver I mentioned, and also to my station chief. How could they bring these women back to their county capitals, and tell their parents and friends that this was their wife, a peasant girl? On the other hand, it was impossible to keep that squirming thing under control, and we'd happily watch ourselves slide into the abyss just to give it five seconds of pleasure. The first girl wrote me a note saying she'd never go out with anyone like me again; I made sure to keep the note in case she changed her mind. The second girl was worse: she helped me make my bed every day, did my laundry and made sure I was eating well. She loved me. And I had nothing but my lust that cut me like a knife. For quite some time I thought I'd never escape from that tender trap. I thought I'd stay with her, and have children, and die like a frog in a well. I couldn't bring myself to say: I want to break up. Or: I don't really like you.

She was called Lifang. She left her job in Beijing and came back wearing a pretty raincoat, looking like a flower at the foot of a wall. The sunlight gleamed on her skin, white and a little plump, like a mound of snow. She opened a new hair salon a few days after she arrived, and the existing salon couldn't compete. We ended up together naturally, going for a stroll in the mountains on an excessively sunny day. The rapeseed flowers were in bloom on the col, and the whole world was crowded with a luxuriant yellow. Her father was a local and worked in some office, but her mother was a peasant woman. She'd never had a proper government position, and by the looks of it never would – she could only do a little business for herself. One day she told me, with a clandestine pleasure: 'I've got an urban registration, too.' For some reason I was choked with sudden sorrow. Peasants often buy themselves urban housing registrations, just so their children can build upon their own success. But I still can't take you back to the county capital. I looked at her without saying a word.

Towards the end of our relationship, she moved the big mirror from her salon into my room, giving me a fright.

'Are you closing the salon?'

'Yes. I'm giving it up – I can't stop thinking of you.'

'Fool.'

I picked up the mirror and headed back to her salon, and she followed behind, crying and shouting, 'You're leaving me!' The people on the street all turned to look, and I shouted, 'I'm not! I'm not!' I would have liked to have slapped her. But I softened in the end. I'd never seen anyone weep so many tears – her face actually seemed to grow thinner. But once her fragrance had again filled my room and my bed, I slid back into despair. I would be with this woman forever. My whole life. I essentially stopped talking to her.

She said: 'Get up and have a drink of water.'

I said: 'Mmmh.'

She said: 'It'll get cold.'

I said: 'Mmmh.'

She said: 'I'll hold the cup for you.'

I said: 'Mmmh.'

She said: 'You'll have to open your mouth.'

I said: 'Mmmh.'

She said: 'What's wrong with you?'

I said: 'Mmmh.'

She said: 'Are you leaving me?'

I said: 'Mmmh.'

In the end, the callow young girl took the advice of someone older and tried one last trick to save the love that I'd let grow cold. For several days in a row she sat on the back of a motorcycle belonging to a fellow who'd returned from working elsewhere, her face pressed against his shoulder, her eyes closed tenderly, as they drove back and forth along the hundred-metre-long street. I sat in the doorway of the police station, reading the newspaper as I always did. It was a roaring touring cycle, with continuously variable transmission and an electric starter, far better than anything we had at the station. Everyone on the street – shop owners and customers and the merely idle – watched as the unregistered vehicle swaggered back and forth in front of the police station. Normally, anyone trying that would have been pulled over and fined.

I was a nervous wreck. I was terrified of what might happen, but also wanted to get it over with – like a child waiting to get an injection. Everyone could see the anxiety on my face. A police officer's woman was going with some young buck. I would sit there all day, until at last I got up silently and went inside, locking the gate. On my last night, the station chief asked me, with the benevolence of a father bidding farewell to a grown son, if I'd like a drink.

'No,' I said firmly.

I bolted down my meal, then tossed my luggage in the jeep. Wang came over and said, 'It was all thanks to me.'

'Right,' I said. 'All thanks to you.'

I knew it was Wang who'd given her the bad advice. Make him jealous, and he'll treat you better. As the jeep emerged from the yard behind the station I was afraid she'd be there, blocking our way. But she never appeared, until at last the jeep entered soundlessly onto the highway. The broken-down thing required constant pit stops, and each time it started hacking and wheezing I worried she'd catch up with us on the back of that motorcycle, sobbing at me: What will I do once you're gone? What will I do?

Luckily the jeep never actually conked out, and we gradually drew farther away, farther than she'd have the courage to follow. When we finally reached the asphalt the sky was completely dark, but I felt beams of radiance bathing my face. I was finally returning from the end of the world. A few days later, in the county capital, I got a phone call from her. She just wept and told me how much she loved me. I said, What were you doing with another man, then? She wept all the harder, and I could imagine her on the other end, shaking her head repeatedly. As she did she cried: No, it wasn't like that.

'So what was it like?'

'That was my cousin driving the bike.'

I was struck dumb, but recovered quickly. I began some witless nattering that floated from my mouth without passing through my brain. I no longer feared that she would entrap me; my heart would not soften. This would be the end of our story. ∎

AUTHOR'S NOTE: *Some names have been changed.*

A WALK TO KOBE

Haruki Murakami

TRANSLATED FROM THE JAPANESE BY PHILIP GABRIEL

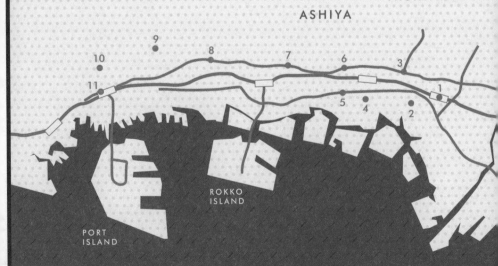

I

In May of 1997, two years after the massive earthquake in Kobe, I hit upon the idea of taking a leisurely, solitary walk from Nishinomiya to Sannomiya in downtown Kobe. I happened to be staying in Kyoto at the time for work, and continued on to Nishinomiya. On the map it's about fifteen kilometres west from there to Kobe. Not exactly a stone's throw away, but not such a gruelling distance, and besides, I'm a pretty confident walker.

I was born in Kyoto, but soon afterwards my family moved to Shukugawa, a neighbourhood in Nishinomiya. And not long after that we moved again, closer to Kobe, to Ashiya, where I spent most of my teenage years. My high school was in the hills above the city, so naturally downtown Kobe was where I headed when I wanted to have a good time, specifically around Sannomiya. I became a typical *Hanshin-kan boy*, the term referring to the area that lies between Osaka and Kobe. Back then – and probably nowadays as well – this was a great place to grow up. It's quiet and laid-back, with an open, relaxed feeling about it, and it's blessed with the ocean, mountains and a large city nearby. I loved going to concerts, hunting for cheap paperbacks in used bookstores, hanging out in jazz cafes, and enjoying Art Theatre Guild new-wave films. My favourite look at the time? VAN jackets, of course.

But then I moved to Tokyo for college, got married and started working, and seldom travelled back to this strip of land between Osaka and Kobe. There were times I'd return, of course, but as soon as I finished what I had to do I'd always hop on the bullet train and head straight back to Tokyo. I had a busy life, and I spent a lot of time abroad. And there were a couple of personal reasons as well. Some people are constantly being pulled back to their home town, while others feel like they can never go back. In most cases it's as if fate separates the two groups, and it has little to do with how strong your feelings are towards the place. Like it or not, I seem to belong to the second group.

For years my parents lived in Ashiya, but when the Hanshin Earthquake hit in January 1995, their house was too damaged to stay in and they soon moved to Kyoto. So, apart from all the memories I'd stored up for myself (my valuable property), there was no longer any actual connection between me and the Hanshin-kan area. Strictly speaking, it's not my home town any more. I feel a deep sense of loss at this fact, as if the axis of my memories is faintly, but audibly, creaking within me. It's a physical sensation.

Maybe it's exactly *because* of that that I wanted to take a walk there, alert and attentive to what I might discover. Perhaps I wanted to see for myself how this *home town* I'd lost all obvious connections with would appear to me now. How much of a shadow (or a shadow of a shadow) of myself I would discover there?

I also wanted to see what effect the Hanshin Earthquake had had on the town I grew up in. I visited Kobe several times after the quake, and was frankly shocked by the extent of damage. But now, some two years later, when the town seemed finally to have righted itself, I wanted to see with my own eyes what transformations had taken place – what this awful violence had stolen from the town, and what it had left behind. There had to be at least some connection, I felt, with who I am now.

Clad in rubber-soled walking shoes, shouldering a backpack with a notebook and small camera, I got off at the train at Nishinomiya station and set off at a leisurely pace towards the west. The weather was so bright and sunny I wore sunglasses. The first place I came to was the shopping area near the south exit of the station. In elementary

school I often used to ride my bike over there to buy things. The city
library was nearby, too, and whenever I had time I'd hang out there
and pore through every young adult book I could lay my hands on.
There was also a craft shop close by where I stocked up on plastic
models. So this place brought back a rush of memories.

I hadn't been here for a long time, and the shopping area had
changed almost beyond recognition. How much of this was due to
the normal changes over time, and how much was because of the
physical devastation brought on by the earthquake, I really couldn't
say. Even so, the scars left by the earthquake were plain to see. Where
buildings had collapsed, vacant lots now dotted the area like so
many missing teeth, with prefab temporary stores in between as if
to connect them all. Summer grass grew in the roped-off vacant lots,
and the asphalt streets were filled with ominous cracks. Compared
to the downtown shopping district of Kobe, which the world had
focused on, and which had rapidly been rebuilt after the quake, the
blank spaces here struck me as somehow heavy and dull, with a quiet
depth to them. Of course this wasn't only true of the Nishinomiya
shopping district. There must be many places around Kobe that still
bear the same sort of wounds, but that are mostly forgotten.

Past the shopping district and across the main street is Ebisu
Shrine. It's a very large shrine, with thick woods within its precincts.
When I was a small child, my friends and I loved to play here, and it
hurt to see the visible scars there now. Most of the large stone lights
lining the Hanshin highway were missing the topmost lantern part.
These were scattered on the ground below, like heads lopped off by
a sharp sword. The remaining bases had become a row of senseless,
purposeless stone statues, solemnly silent, like symbols from a dream.

The old stone bridge across the pond where I used to catch shrimp
as a child (using a simple technique: I would tie a string around an
empty bottle, put in noodle powder as bait, lower it into the water
and the shrimp would go into the bottle and then I would pull it up)
had collapsed and remained that way. The water in the pond was
dark and muddy and turtles of indiscriminate ages lay sprawled on

dry rocks, basking in the sun, their minds no doubt bereft of any thoughts. Terrible destruction was in evidence all around, as if the area was some ancient ruins. Only the deep woods were the same as I remembered from childhood, dark and still, beyond time.

I sat down in the shrine grounds under the early-summer sun, and gazed around again at the surroundings, trying to get used to what I was seeing. Absorbing and accepting this scenery as naturally as I could, mentally and viscerally. Trying to remember how I was back then. But this was all going to take a long time, as you might imagine.

2

I strode on from Nishinomiya to Shukugawa. It was not yet noon, but sunny enough that, walking briskly, I started to perspire. I didn't need a map to tell me roughly where I was, but I had no memory of the individual streets. I must have walked down these streets hundreds of times, but now I was drawing a complete blank. Why couldn't I recall them? It was strange. I felt bewildered, as if I'd come home to find all the furniture replaced.

The reason was soon clear to me. Places that used to be empty lots weren't empty any more, and places that hadn't been empty now were – like photo negatives and positives replacing each other. In most cases the former were empty lots that were now residences, the latter where old houses had been destroyed in the earthquake. These before-and-after images had a synergistic effect, adding a fictitious wash to my memories of how the town used to be.

The old house I had lived in near Shukugawa was gone, replaced by a row of town houses. And the grounds of the nearby high school were filled with temporary housing put up for survivors of the quake. Where my friends and I used to play baseball, the people who lived in these prefab shelters had hung their laundry and futons out to air, in what now seemed like a tight, cramped space. Try as I might to find vestiges of the past, there were almost none. The water in the river still flowed as clean and pure as before, but it gave me an odd sensation to see how the riverbed was now neatly lined with concrete.

I walked on for a while in the direction of the sea and stopped by a local sushi shop. It was a Sunday afternoon, and they were busy with takeout orders. The young assistant who'd gone out on deliveries didn't come back for a long time, and the owner was hard-pressed to keep up with the phone calls. A typical scene you'd find anywhere in Japan. I waited for my order to come, sipping a beer and half watching the TV. The governor of Hyogo prefecture was talking with someone on a show about how post-quake reconstruction was going. I'm trying to remember now exactly what he said, but for the life of me can't recall a single word.

As a child, when I climbed the banks of the river, the sea was spread out right in front of me, with nothing blocking the view. I used to go swimming there in the summer. I loved the ocean and loved to swim. I went fishing, too, and took my dog for a walk there every day. Sometimes I just liked to sit down and do nothing. And sometimes I'd sneak out of the house at night, go to the sea with my friends and gather driftwood and light a bonfire. I loved the smell of the sea, its far-off roar, and all that it brought with it.

But now the sea isn't there any more. They cut down the mountains, hauled all the dirt off to the sea with trucks and conveyor belts and filled it in. With both the mountains and sea so close by, this area is perfect for that kind of construction work. Neat little residential communities have sprung up where the mountains used to be, and similarly neat little residential communities have popped up on the landfill. All this happened after I moved to Tokyo, during the era of high growth in Japan, when the country was in the throes of a nationwide construction boom.

I own a house now in a town on the seashore in Kanagawa prefecture near Tokyo, and travel back and forth between there and Tokyo. Unfortunately, or *very* unfortunately, I should say, this seaside town reminds me more of my home town than my home town does.

The area has green mountains, and a wonderful swimming beach. I want to preserve these as best I can, because once natural scenery is gone, it's gone forever. Once violence caused by humans is unleashed, it can never be reversed.

Past the banks of the river, the area around what used to be the Koroen seaside resort had been filled in to make a kind of cosy little cove, or pond. Windsurfers were there, doing their best to catch the wind. Just to the west, on what was Ashiya beach, stands a row of high-rise apartment buildings, like so many blank monoliths. On the shore, some families that have driven there in their station wagons and minivans are using small propane tanks to have a barbecue. So-called *outdoor* activities. They're grilling meat, fish and vegetables, and the whitish smoke silently rises like a beacon into the sky on this happy Sunday scene. There's hardly a cloud in the sky. An almost perfect May tableau. Still, as I sit there on the concrete bank and gaze at where the real sea used to be, everything here, like a tyre leaking air, slowly, and quietly, loses its sense of reality.

In the midst of this placid scene it's hard to deny the vestiges of violence. That's how it struck me. A part of those violent tendencies lies hidden right below our feet, while another part is hidden within us. One is a metaphor for the other. Or perhaps they are interchangeable. Lying here, asleep, like a pair of animals having the same dream.

I crossed a small river and went into Ashiya. I walked past my old junior high school, past the house I used to live in, and came to the Ashiya train station. A poster in the station announced a game at 2 p.m. that day at Koshien Stadium in Osaka between the Hanshin Tigers and Yakult Swallows baseball teams. Seeing it, I had the sudden urge to go. I made a quick change of plans and jumped on the train. The game had just begun, so if I went now, I thought, I should be there in time for the third inning. I could resume my walk tomorrow.

Koshien Stadium had changed little from when I was child. Like I'd stumbled into a time warp, I felt a keen nostalgic sense of not belonging – an odd turn of phrase, admittedly. About the only things that had changed were the lack of hawkers shouldering polka-dot tanks of Calpis, selling the fermented milk drink (seems like there aren't many people in the world who drink Calpis any more), and the outfield scoreboard, which was now electronic (and hard to decipher during the day). But the colour of the dirt on the field was the same as before, as was the green of the grass, and the Hanshin fans were as famously boisterous as ever. Earthquakes, revolutions, wars and centuries can come and go, but Hanshin fans are eternal.

The game turned out to be a pitcher's duel between Kawajiri and Takatsu, with Hanshin winning 1–0. You might think the one-run difference meant it was a thrilling game but it wasn't, not by any stretch of the imagination. If anything, it was a highlight-free sort of game. To put it even more bluntly, a game not worth seeing. Especially for those of us in the outfield seats. As the sun got stronger we grew horribly thirsty. I had a few cold beers and, predictably, dozed off on the bleachers. When I woke up I had totally lost track of where I was. (Where the hell *am* I? I wondered.) The shadows from the floodlights had meandered in my direction, nearly reaching me.

3

I checked into a new little hotel in Kobe. Most of the guests were groups of young women. I'm sure you can picture the kind of hotel I'm talking about. The next morning I got up at six and took the pre-rush-hour train to Ashiyagawa station, and restarted my mini walking tour. Unlike the day before, the sky was covered with clouds, the air a bit chilly. The weather report in the paper confidently predicted rain in the afternoon (and of course they were spot on. In the evening I got drenched).

In the morning paper I'd bought at Sannomiya station there was also an update on an assault on two young girls in Suma New Town (another new place built by slicing off mountain tops, I imagined; I'd never heard of it). One of them had died. Police were calling it a random attack, and had no clues, and residents with small children were frightened. This was before the awful murder of Jun Hase, an eleven-year-old boy, took place in Kobe. At any rate, it was a horrible, gruesome, pointless attack targeting elementary-school children. I rarely read the newspaper and hadn't even known about the attack.

I remember sensing a matter-of-fact, yet deep and uncanny undertone lurking between the lines of the article. As I folded up the paper, a thought suddenly struck me. *A man walking around by himself in the middle of the day on a weekday might appear pretty suspicious.* This shadow of renewed violence underscored even more my sense of being a *foreign element* here. Like I was an uninvited guest who'd blundered into a place I didn't belong.

I walked along a road in the foothills where the railroad line runs, taking little detours as I made my way west, and in about thirty minutes had entered Ashiya. It is a long, narrow town running north and south. Walk east or west and you've soon left it. On either side of the road there were empty lots here, too, left over from the earthquake, and a few deserted houses tilting to one side. The soil in the Hanshin-kan area differs from that in Tokyo. It's a sandy mountainous area, so the earth is smooth and whitish, which made the empty lots stand out all the more. The area was thick with green summer weeds, making the contrast even more striking. I pictured a large surgical scar on the skin of someone close to me, an image that sent a physical, stabbing pain right through me, a pain not tethered to time or place.

Naturally there was more than just vacant lots covered in weeds. I did run across several construction sites. I imagine that in less than a year there will be rows of newly built houses here, so many I probably wouldn't recognize the place. Brand-new roof tiles, sparkling brilliantly in the fresh rays of the sun. By then there might be nothing left in common between the scenery here and me as a person. (Most likely there *won't* be.) Between us (probably) stands a forced divide exposed by an overwhelming destructive device, namely the earthquake. I gazed up at the sky, breathed in the slightly cloudy morning air, and thought about this land that had made me into the person I am, and about the person whom this land had made. About the sort of things we have no control over.

When I arrived at Okamoto station, the next station over, I thought I'd stop by a coffee shop – any place would do – and order their set breakfast. I hadn't eaten anything all morning. But none of the coffee shops were open yet. It wasn't that kind of town, I remembered. Reluctantly, I bought a CalorieMate energy bar at a Lawson's beside the road, sat on a park bench and silently ate it, washing it down with a can of coffee. I used the time to jot down notes on what I'd seen on the journey so far. After a short break I pulled out the paperback copy of Hemingway's *The Sun Also Rises* from my pocket and took up where I'd left off. I'd read the novel in high school, and had happened to start it again in bed in the hotel and had become totally lost in the story. I wonder why I never realized before what a great novel it is. This realization gave me an odd sensation. I guess my mind must have been elsewhere back then.

There was no breakfast service to be found at the next station, Mikage, either, so I went on silently trudging along the train tracks, lost in dreams of strong, steaming hot coffee and slices of thick, buttered toast. As before, I passed a number of empty lots and construction sites. Several Mercedes-Benz E-Class sedans glided by, taking children to school or the station, I imagine. The cars didn't have a single smudge or a scratch. Like symbols have no substance, and the flow of time no goal. All unconnected to the earthquake, or to violence. Most likely.

In front of Rokko station I made a small concession, went into a McDonald's, ordered an Egg McMuffin set (360 yen) and was able finally to appease the hunger that had been growling inside me like the roar of the sea. I decided to take a thirty-minute break. It was now 9 a.m. Going inside a McDonald's at 9 a.m., I felt like I'd been absorbed into a huge McDonald's-esque imaginary reality. Or become part of some mass unconscious. But really, all that surrounded me was my own individual reality. Obviously. For better or for worse, it's just that that individualism had, temporarily, no place to go.

I'd managed to make it this far, so I decided to climb the steep slope that led to my old high school. A light sheen of sweat broke out on my forehead. In high school I always rode a packed bus to school, but now I walked the same road under my own steam. In the spacious playing field that had been carved out of the mountain slopes, girl students were playing handball as part of their gym class. There was an unearthly quiet all around, except for the occasional shouts of the girls. It was so completely still it felt like I'd stumbled into a level of space I shouldn't be in. Why this utter silence?

I gazed at Kobe harbour, sparkling leadenly far below, and listened carefully, hoping to pick up some echoes from the past, but nothing came to me. Just the sounds of silence. That's all. But what are you going to do? We're talking about things that happened over thirty years ago.

Over thirty years ago. There is one thing I can say for certain: the older a person gets, the lonelier he becomes. It's true for everyone. But maybe that isn't wrong. What I mean is, in a sense our lives are nothing more than a series of stages to help us get used to loneliness. That being the case, there's no reason to complain. And besides, who would we complain to, anyway?

4

I stood up, left the high school, and started rather apathetically down the long slope (I was getting a little fatigued). I continued without a break to the Shin Kobe station, the one where the bullet trains stop. From here I could get to my destination, Sannomiya, in one go.

I had extra time, so out of sheer curiosity I stopped inside the New Kobe Oriental Hotel, a mammoth, newly opened hotel near the station. I sank back on a sofa in the cafe lounge and finally got my first decent cup of coffee of the day. I lowered my backpack, removed my sunglasses, took a deep breath and gave my legs a rest.

It occurred to me that I needed to use the facilities, so I went and relieved myself for the first time since leaving my hotel that morning. Then I sat back, ordered a refill of coffee, and took a look around me. The hotel was dreadfully spacious, worlds apart from the old Kobe Oriental Hotel near the harbour (a nice, cosy-sized hotel now closed because of the earthquake). Calling this new hotel deserted rather than spacious might be closer to reality. It was kind of like a pyramid with not enough mummies. I don't mean to quibble, but it's not the sort of place where I'd like to stay.

A few months later there was a yakuza-related shooting in the very same lounge, and two people were killed. Of course I had no way of knowing something like that would take place there, but once again I happened to pass by, with a gap of time separating us, a shadow of violence to come. Call it coincidence, but it still made me feel weird, like the past, the present and the future were all flashing back and forth together on an overpass above me.

Why are we being exposed to such profound and continual violence? Four months after this little walking trip, as I sit at my desk and write these words, I can't help but wonder. Even putting aside the Kobe region, I feel like one act of violence is destined (in reality or metaphorically) to lead directly to another. Is there some kind of generational inevitability to this? Or is it just chance and nothing more?

The Hanshin Earthquake took place while I was living in the United States, and two months after that came the sarin gas attack on the Tokyo subway. I found this a very suggestive chain of events. That summer I returned to Japan, and soon after began interviewing survivors of the sarin attack. One year later I published *Underground*. What I was seeking in that book, what I wanted to write about – what I, myself, really wanted to know more about – was the violence in our society that lies hidden right beneath us. About the violence that's there as a latent possibility, and the possibility that actually reveals itself in the form of violence, all of which we tend to forget exists. That's why I didn't choose the victimizers in the attack to interview, but the victims.

As I walked silently along for two days from Nishinomiya to Kobe, these ideas kept spinning around in my head. As I made my way through the earthquake's shadow I kept asking myself: *What was the sarin gas attack on the subway all about?* At the same time, as I dragged along the shadow of the sarin gas attack, I wondered: *What was the Hanshin Earthquake?* To me, the two events weren't separate and discrete; unravelling one might help unravel the other. This was simultaneously a physical and a psychological issue. In other words, the psychological is itself the physical. And I had to create my own sort of corridor connecting the two.

I could add an even more critical question to the mix, namely: *What can I do about it?*

Sorry to say, I still haven't found a clear, logical answer to these questions. I haven't arrived at any definite destination. All I'm able to do at this point is, through my uncertain prose, serve up in an anticlimactic vessel the actual path my thoughts (and my gaze and legs) led me to. I hope you will understand this. Ultimately I'm the kind of person who can only make progress through moving my legs, moving my body, through a step-by-step, halting, physical process. It takes time. A miserably long amount of time. I just hope it won't be too late.

I finally arrived back in Sannomiya. By this time I was starting to smell pretty rank. It wasn't such a long distance, though further than your typical morning stroll. In the hotel room I took a hot shower, washed my hair and gulped down a cold bottle of mineral water from the fridge. I took out a fresh change of clothes from my bag. Navy-blue polo shirt, blue cotton sports coat and beige chinos. My legs were a bit swollen, but there was nothing I could do about it. Just like I couldn't extract the vague questions that lay dull and unresolved in my head.

There wasn't anything in particular I wanted to do, so I went to see a film that caught my eye, one starring Tom Cruise. Not all that moving a film, but not so bad, either. I just took a rest, passing the time. Two hours of my life passed by – not so movingly, but not so badly, either. Evening was coming on as I exited the theatre, and I strolled up towards the hills to a little restaurant. I sat at the counter, ordered a seafood pizza and a draught beer. I was the only customer who was by himself. Maybe it was just my imagination, but everyone else there seemed really happy. The couples looked contented, and a group of men and women were laughing uproariously. Some days are just like that.

The seafood pizza they brought me had a little paper tag on it announcing that *This pizza you are about to enjoy is the 958,816th pizza made by our restaurant.* I couldn't follow. 958,816? What sort of message was I supposed to read into this? When I was young, I often used to come to this place with my girlfriend, down a few cold beers, and eat a freshly baked pizza with the same kind of numbered tag. We'd talk about our future. And of all the predictions we made then, not a single one came true. But this was a long, long time ago. Back when there was still a sea here, back when there were mountains.

Not that there aren't still sea and mountains here. Of course there are. What I'm talking about is a different sea, and different mountains. Different from the ones here now. As I sip my second beer, I flip open my paperback copy of *The Sun Also Rises* and pick up where I left off. The lost story of a lost generation. I'm quickly lured back into their world.

When I finally leave the restaurant, it's raining, as predicted, and I get wet. Wretchedly wet, soaked to the bone. But by this point it's too much trouble to buy an umbrella. ■

Compass Plant

One sprig should do, in a wayfarer's satchel,
to assist in losing all bearings
until you're standing
where the road stops you,

as a road should never do,
closed off even as it continues
towards its green retinue
in a long grey disguise.

Think about it, you're diverted,
as if you'd seen into the earth,
drawn like a magnet
through a field of old stories

where borders are buried
to a Rhymer's Stone –
take it as a blessing,
with no thought for the road

SEESTÜCK

Steffi Klenz

The following portraits are based on photographs of travellers, explorers and seamen who were lost in open waters, and whose bodies were never recovered. Artist Steffi Klenz recaptured these forgotten faces from digital stills and then exposed the physical negatives to corrosive seawater bacteria, causing the surfaces to bloom and ripple, echoing and memorializing their owners' salty erasure. From Joshua Slocum, the first man to sail single-handedly around the world, in the 1890s, who later disappeared in 1909 from his yacht *Spray*, to adventurer Andrew McAuley, who disappeared while attempting to kayak 1,600 kilometres across the Tasman Sea in 2007, Klenz exhumes these lost souls from the depths and offers us the after-image of their ravaging by the high seas. ∎

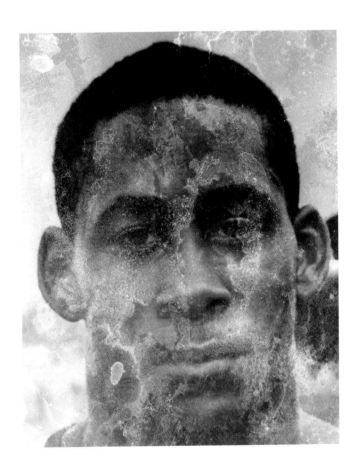

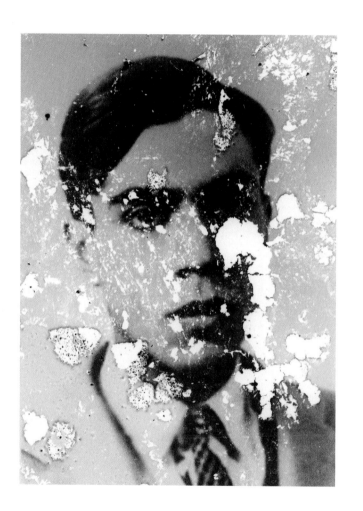

Take the trip

Have *Granta* delivered to your door
four times a year and save up to
29% on the cover price.

Subscribe now by completing the form overleaf,
visiting granta.com or calling toll-free* 845-267-3031
*Toll-free rate only applicable to US callers.

US
$48

Canada
$56

Latin America
$68

'Provides enough to satisfy
the most rabid appetite
for good writing and hard thinking'
– *Washington Post*

GRANTA.COM

GRANTA
THE MAGAZINE OF NEW WRITING

SUBSCRIPTION FORM FOR US, CANADA AND LATIN AMERICA

Yes, I would like to take out a subscription to *Granta*.

GUARANTEE: If I am ever dissatisfied with my *Granta* subscription, I will simply notify you, and you will send me a complete refund or credit my credit card, as applicable, for all un-mailed issues.

YOUR DETAILS

MR / MISS / MRS / DR ....

NAME ....

ADDRESS ....

....

CITY .... STATE ....

ZIP CODE .... COUNTRY ....

EMAIL ....

☐ Please check this box if you do not wish to receive special offers from *Granta*

☐ Please check this box if you do not wish to receive offers from organizations selected by *Granta*

YOUR PAYMENT DETAILS

1 year subscription: ☐ US: $48   ☐ Canada: $56   ☐ Latin America: $68

3 year subscription: ☐ US: $120   ☐ Canada: $144   ☐ Latin America: $180

Enclosed is my check for $ _____ made payable to *Granta*.

Please charge my: ☐ Visa   ☐ MasterCard   ☐ Amex

Card No. ☐☐☐☐☐☐☐☐☐☐☐☐☐☐☐☐

Exp. ☐☐☐☐

Security Code ☐☐☐☐☐

SIGNATURE .... DATE ....

Please mail this order form with your payment instructions to:

Granta Publications
PO Box 359
Congers NY 10920-0359

Or call 845-267-3031
Or visit GRANTA.COM for details

Source code: BUS124PM

THE BEST HOTEL

Sonia Faleiro

I

The village elder had recommended the hotel. He called it the best hotel in Amni. Or perhaps he said it was the Best Hotel in Amni; either way he was wrong. It was neither. It was a few kilometres outside Amni village, in the closest town, on the one street. There were dozens of stray dogs about, and they rooted in the piles of garbage accumulated outside the shops, even the ones that sold coils of rope and farm implements.

A piece of paper on the hotel door read: LEARN ENGLISH LIKE AMERICAN. On another piece of paper, set too high to see clearly, was scrawled the name of the hotel. From outside, the reception appeared cave-like. Inside, a man at an office table stared nervously into a guest register.

'One person?' he asked. Yes, I replied. He looked over my shoulder at my guide, Ramesh, standing by the door texting. The driver was outside, waiting to drive back with Ramesh to Amni where they had both decided to spend the night.

How free they were. They could spend an entire night in the open. They would sit by the fire talking and smoking beedis, chewing tobacco and drinking country liquor with the village men. When they got hungry one of the men would call out to his wife, 'Listen, is food ready?' And she would emerge promptly with enough dal and rotis for everyone. It would be plain, perhaps even watery dal, without even an onion or chilli for punch, but it would be warm and filling. They would sleep by the fire, swaddled in shawls, safe as only men can be. In the morning they would shit by the pond, wash in the pond and then order little glasses of chai at the tea shop where the one who knew the alphabet would read aloud the newspaper that had made it to the village. When it was time for something substantial, one of them would call out to his wife, 'Listen, is breakfast ready?'

He won't be staying, I said. The man didn't believe me, but he took my money anyway, and handed me a key. 'Take madam to the room,' he said, seemingly to no one.

From under the table emerged a head and then, on all fours, came the rest of a teenage boy. He wore a waiter's uniform, quite dirty and torn, and was pleased at the unexpected break. He straightened himself, threw aside the cloth he'd been mopping with and bounded up the stairs, as though afraid the man would change his mind. At the top of the floor he lifted his voice and called, 'Toilet-cum-bathroom,' as if it were someone's name. The shared toilets and the cubicles for bucket baths were actually down the corridor, but perhaps they were too confining, for here the men were, in the hallway, rubbing their freshly washed hair and brushing their teeth as they padded up and down in their towels. A few of them leaned against the railings that looked down on the reception, dripping water and dropping demands – 'Thali!' 'Beer!' 'Plate pakora!'

We continued our climb, and on the second floor the teenager announced, 'Rooms,' and that was all there was – rooms lined like books on a shelf, room numbers scrawled in chalk.

When we reached the third floor he grew tall. 'Bed-cum-baths!' he said with pride.

My room was large and, by the standards of Amni, luxurious. There was a bed, table and chairs, even a small TV. Two young men – teenagers really – were changing the linen. They tucked in grey-stained sheets and smoothed down a thin, ripped bedspread, running their hands gently over it. One of them offered to bring me water; the other asked what I would like to eat for dinner. I was touched by their politeness, but distracted by a strong, sweet smell that hit me with the force of a migraine.

What is that smell? I asked.

'Nothing,' one of them said.

Really? I replied.

'This is our best room,' he said, disappointed.

The teenagers left unhappy and I was sorry, but I still locked the door behind them and sought out the source of the smell. I checked under the bed; the floor was filthy and clotted with dust. I peered into the bathroom. The Indian-style latrine was soiled, but even that smell, of a Mumbai railway-station toilet, wasn't it. I turned back into the room and threw open the windows.

The night was clear and fresh, but not a single light punctuated the darkness. The shops, the dogs and whatever other animals were growing fat on the trash that threatened to gobble up the town, were now so well concealed that they may as well have not existed.

From where I stood, looking at the town – beyond it the fields, and somewhere out there Amni – I saw only darkness. It could have been a hundred years ago, which was a pleasant enough thought, but what if it remained like this even ten years from now? The possibility that change wouldn't come soon enough to matter to the people who lived there was terrifying. Down below a man cleared his throat and called out clear as a temple bell, '*Jaagte raho!*' The watchman brought down his bamboo stick and demanded, 'Staaay Awake!' He wasn't asking anyone to stay awake; he was reminding himself to be alert. It was a comforting sound that took me back to my childhood in Delhi. Our middle-class neighbourhood used to have a roving watchman too and at night his call lulled me to sleep.

I couldn't bring myself to lie on the linen, so I spread out my shawl and tucked my rucksack under my head. I flipped open my iPad and started watching an American TV show. It made me laugh. Soon, I forgot to be bothered by the nauseating smell. I drifted. The screen swam, it churned, the laughter of children, women inside their huts, men by the fire, the boy on a bus, his nose at the gates, his small body buried under an avalanche of handbags.

I was on the trail of child traffickers. My journey had brought me to Amni village in Bihar, a part of the world in which children were made to do the work of adults, while adults lived off their earnings.

The watchman called out. 'Stay awake,' he said. 'BE ALERT.'

R amesh and I had found Amni by chance, or so it seemed.
Searching for a place to eat breakfast, we happened to pass a
dhaba – a cheap roadside restaurant – with a note taped prominently
to the entrance. It said, in Hindi: WE DO NOT EMPLOY CHILD
LABOURERS. Intrigued, I jumped out of the jeep and readied my
camera. But I had barely brought it up to my face when I felt a hard
tap on my shoulder. A hunkering man with a handlebar moustache
looked down at me. 'What are you doing?' he demanded.

Who are you? I asked.

'Police,' he said. He wasn't in uniform. 'Why are you taking
photographs?'

Because it's my job, I told him.

Ramesh had gone inside the dhaba to ask for a menu, but now he
bounded out, the dhaba owner at his heels. 'Officer sahib,' Ramesh
smiled widely, his hands folded in greeting. 'How are you? So nice to
see you. Meet madam. She has come from outside. She is a journalist,
new to Bihar.'

The man gave him a cold look. 'She is from foreign,' he said. 'But
you are clearly from here. You should keep control.'

This is a good thing, I said, gesturing at the note. I want to write
about it.

The man wouldn't look at me. 'Be careful,' he warned Ramesh. 'If
anything goes wrong, I will find you.'

The policeman, if he was that, walked off. The dhaba owner
looked busy. Ramesh shrugged. 'Bihari peoples are very sensitize,' he
offered in English.

After breakfast, we decided to take a look around the village. It
was neatly laid out and clean, but the huts were of the poorest sort,
shaped of straw and bamboo poles. Smoke rose from cooking fires.
Goats grazed freely. At the periphery of a green pond little children
squatted, chatting animatedly as they passed stool. This isn't an

unusual sight in India, and I wouldn't have thought twice about it except for what I saw just a few feet ahead.

Standing against a hut, straight as pencils, was a row of white ceramic Indian-style latrines. They had been filled with mud and were sprouting flowers. Someone enterprising had decided to use them as planters.

Still ahead were more children, as many as two dozen, running around like they were in a playground, except that they were in an open-air shed packed with cows and buffaloes. This was where we met the boy.

He was twelve or thirteen, engulfed in the hand-me-downs of a full-grown man, perhaps his father. An enormous leather belt went around his waist not once, but twice. He wore what looked to be his father's shoes as well, or it would be more accurate to say they wore him, for they were so big he didn't walk in them as much as shuffle them along.

He minded the younger children in a cheerful, if careless way. 'Look at you!' he said, as a toddler tripped and fell into a pile of manure. 'Are you even girls?' he scolded two little girls poking each other in the face with sticks.

It was Ramesh who asked him the question, as if it were the most obvious thing to ask a child. And perhaps it was in rural Bihar, the local equivalent of 'What's your name?' or 'How old are you?'

'Do you work?' Ramesh asked.

'Why?' said the boy. 'Want someone?'

Can we talk to you? I said.

The boy lost interest.

Who put you to work?

'Speak to my mother,' he said.

The boy didn't look around for his mother, nor did he tell us where to find her. Instead he said, 'I go with my uncle.'

Who gives *him* permission?

'For what?'

To put you to work?

'What will I do here?' he cried shrilly.

What do you do there?

'Everything. One time I worked in a rice mill. Another time he took me to a carpet factory. And one more time he put me in charge of sewing the straps on ladies' handbags.'

A toddler, completely naked, giggled when he heard the word 'bag'. He sashayed through the manure as though he was carrying a handbag, his feet leaving behind tiny imprints.

The boy narrowed his eyes. 'Watch it,' he growled. 'Or I'll shove you into the latrine.'

The latrines have flowers in them, I reminded him.

He burst out laughing. 'Of course they do,' he said. 'What else would we use them for? Don't we have a pond?'

We had driven all night to get here from Jharkhand, a state that was once a part of Bihar, and was staggering under the same burdens – primarily poverty and caste discord.

Jharkhand has a smooth, wide highway, but like many parts of the state, parts of the highway have no power. To compensate, drivers switch on their high beams. They honk urgently. Trucks and buses make a sport of overtaking each other, so there are often two enormous vehicles hurtling towards you, one directly in your lane.

We were in the smallest car on the road. It didn't even have working lights, but this fact, instead of humbling our driver, prodded him to a maniac competitiveness. He hunched over the steering wheel and slammed on the gas. 'I do this all the time,' he cried. 'It's my job!'

After an hour or so, the traffic faded. But for the moon, we would have been steeped in darkness. It gleamed clear as a torch on the road, illuminating the forest on either side, revealing pathways and ponds. It was a moment of unexpected beauty and I was grateful for it.

Then Ramesh rolled up his window. 'Watch for Naxalites,' he warned.

In Jharkhand, we watched constantly for Naxalites. The leftist extremists planted bombs on buses, trains and bridges, but they also struck in the dark, robbing and killing people before melting into the nearby forests or mountains. To be in 'Naxalite territory', as we were now, was to be ready for ambush. If that happened I was to step up with my media credentials, making clear I was worth keeping alive.

What would Ramesh do?

'I will hug my comrades and invite them to dinner in my home,' said the innocent.

So we rolled up the windows, switched off the radio and accelerated, speeding down the highway. We willed the border to come. But what we saw ahead could not be blamed on the Naxalites.

Traffic had backed up, and the dozens of buses and trucks that had raced past us now stalled, deflated. Drivers, all of them men, strolled up and down the highway, shadowy figures grasping cigarettes and cellphones. They passed on the news – there had been an accident. The police and an ambulance had only just arrived.

We parked behind everyone else, and our driver turned to me. 'You wait here,' he said. 'I'll go look.'

Ramesh agreed. 'Wait inside the car until we know what's happening.'

They were afraid for me, and their fear was not unfounded. Women were a reliable target around here, even when it wasn't dark and chaotic with men. But I could not afford to be a captive of their fears, or to succumb to mine. If I did, I would retreat, if not from this place, and this pursuit, then some other. If I did, the men might not win, but I would definitely lose.

So we got out of the car together and started walking to the head of the traffic jam, past the buses and trucks, the accumulations of fractious, fidgety men, the women seemingly secure but still vulnerable behind rolled-up windows. We walked for fifteen minutes.

A policeman said the driver of the motorcycle, in overtaking a bus, had flown into the face of an oncoming truck. The driver was thrown off the motorcycle, and there he was – a misshapen heap, broken but still breathing. He was no more than a teenager. When the truck hit he flew, but the young man sitting behind him was plucked off the bike and dragged along, in the opposite direction. No one got the truck's number plate, or even knew where it was now. But several of us could see the young man.

'Look,' said someone. 'A finger!'

A policeman pounced on it and stuck it in a garbage bag.

With the help of bystanders, using their cellphones for light, the police then gathered up the body parts they could see – a hand, a leg, some unidentifiable bits – and eventually, at the base of a tree down the road, the young man's severed head.

The family members arrived. There were six of them, and they stepped out of their white Maruti van in order of gender. First came the men, and they went straight to the driver of the motorcycle. Then came the women, in salwar kameezes and saris, high heels and glass bangles, and they were still, as though they had expended all their energy in that single step from van to road. If they spoke, or even wept, I didn't hear them – several of the truck drivers had got tired of waiting and they pounded their horns like bullies.

A family member walked over. 'They had gone to buy *mithai*,' he said, with a bewildered expression. 'So many guests had come, but there were no sweets to feed them.'

I had arrived in India three days earlier from San Francisco where I now live. After a night in Bangalore, I flew into Jharkhand to meet a *mukhia*, one of the leaders of a tribal community that lived deep inside a protected forest. I was investigating child labour. According to a UNICEF estimate, India had 28 million child labourers – defined as someone under the age of fourteen performing adult jobs. Some were hidden in plain sight. They served food in dhabas or washed cars in gas stations. The rest were simply hidden – in carpet factories and down coal mines.

I was here because I knew that isolated communities were at great risk from spotters. Spotters were often a child's first contact with a trafficking network.

I hired a jeep and driver, as well as a guide. This was Ramesh, a bony young man with shiny black hair that stuck out from under a green Che Guevara-style cap. He called me 'comrade', and in this way signalled his sympathy for the Naxalites. Ramesh asked if he could invite a friend or two along to enjoy the drive into the forest, but that number quickly multiplied, and suddenly there were six of us crammed into four seats. I was the only woman, but my fellow comrades didn't seem to notice. Summer had just begun, but the sun struck a thousand blows. Squeezed into one another, we sweated helplessly down the backs of our plastic seats.

The comrades hoped to see some deer, but all we saw were silent bands of foragers. Little girls in torn dresses poured yellow mahua flowers into straw baskets. These would be distilled into alcohol and sold in town for five rupees a packet. Women collected scraps of wood for cooking fuel, and two men hacking at a tree threw down their machetes when they saw us and ran away. Cutting trees is illegal in protected areas, and perhaps they mistook us for forest officers. The jeep nosed through the foliage, jerked sloppily over riverbeds, and covered what seemed like fifteen kilometres, before finally coming to a halt under an enormous banyan tree.

The *mukhia* was an immediately impressive woman. She was slight and thirty-something, with a high forehead and a sharp, clever face. She was tying her cellphone to a tree trunk with a piece of rope.

'Trying to catch tower,' she called out, motioning for us to wait.

The lack of 'tower' or connectivity manifested itself in other ways, with grave consequences. The village had a school, but three of the four teachers lived in town. The headmaster lived in Bihar. Although he owned a motorcycle, he couldn't drive it easily through the forest, so he parked it at the forest's edge and walked the rest of the way. He scrambled over rocks, and in the monsoon, rolled up his trouser legs, perched his book bag on his head, and waded through the rivers. It took him three hours to get to the village, essentially performing a triathlon. He was fed up and, like the other teachers, had started to skip work. The children were bored, and one after the other they gave up on the idea of school and joined their parents in digging for scraps of mica in the mineral-rich forest. This way they made themselves useful. When they were done with work, they borrowed their parents' cellphones and listened to Hindi film music around the village well. Or they clustered under the banyan tree and made a game of greeting strangers.

'As they grow older,' said the *mukhia*, 'they know, no matter what their parents say, that it would be better if they were not a burden.'

Children like these are at great risk from spotters – men who identify likely victims for trafficking, and pass on the information to their bosses. A spotter neither sources children directly, nor does he abduct them. He merely learns enough so another member of his crew, whom he may never meet nor even know by name, can decide whether to trick the victim's parents into handing over their child (through the promise of marriage or an apprenticeship) or abduct the child outright.

In Jharkhand, spotters spread like pollen – quietly and widely. And they never linger. A spotter who'd ridden the train up from Chhattisgarh would take the next bus to Bihar. Although he travelled alone, he carried with him the names, faces and addresses of the children he picked out.

I decided to follow the spotters into Bihar.

2

It would be my first time. Bihar, arguably, had the worst reputation of any Indian state. As late as the early 2000s it was consumed with caste wars led by privileged upper-caste landowners claiming that landless, low-caste Dalits – once referred to as Untouchables – were scheming to seize their land.

Private militias ploughed through Dalit villages gunning down men, women and children, many of whom worked for them. One militia, known as the Ranvir Sena, an army named after a mythical hero of upper-caste Brahmins, was linked to the deaths of over two hundred people. The police either supported the killings or ignored them. The Naxalites had mobilized the Dalits to agitate for better treatment, feeding the paranoia that supposedly led to the massacres. Now they fought the militias fiercely on behalf of the Dalits. Bihar was plunged into violent anarchy and the term Bihari, once synonymous with mere poverty, came to mean both hopeless and brutish.

At the peak of the violence, in the 1990s, the state chief minister was a man called Laloo Prasad Yadav. It was under his leadership that the term Jungle Raj, or rule of the jungle, came to be used. In his forties, Yadav had the face of a roguish sprite, with bushy eyebrows and wispy white bangs. He gave interviews in his undershirt while tending to his cows. Yadav played the rustic buffoon, but he was, by all accounts, a cunning and sophisticated politician who grew fat from the rupturing of Bihar. To one of his children's weddings, he is alleged to have invited 25,000 people. His associates walked into car dealerships across the state capital of Patna and drove out with cars they hadn't paid for so they could ferry about the guests. And Hindi film actresses, whose company Yadav was said to enjoy, were expected to dance onstage.

I had no sources in Bihar, but in rural India people are generally happy to talk, especially once the sun sets and there isn't field work to attend to. If the problem was as acute as the *mukhia* had suggested, I would have no trouble hearing about it. Ramesh said if we drove at night, we could be in Bihar by dawn.

It seemed like a good plan.

3

A couple of days into my stay in Bihar, I responded to a knock on my door to find an old man in a lungi with a cup of tea in his hand. I hadn't asked for tea, not at 6 a.m., and after it tasted salty, I thought it best to skip breakfast at the hotel. The room still smelled like old perfume, and the cause was a mystery.

I went down at a more reasonable hour, and into a store out front. A pile of dogs, ribs poking through their coats, gazed up at me as I paid for 200 grams of dry puffed rice – a common breakfast snack. Impulsively, I bought some biscuits as well and spilled them out for the dogs. What a scramble! When I turned back towards the hotel to wait for Ramesh, the dogs padded along noiselessly as though they hoped to go unnoticed. We waited together, until some passers-by, seeing us, thought the dogs had me cornered, and that if only it wasn't for them I would be on my way.

'Huurrr!' cried a man on a bicycle like he was addressing a buffalo.

'*Chal hat!*' said another man who actually *was* walking a buffalo.

A little girl in a school uniform, a brown paper bag of toffees in her hand, paused to enjoy the unfolding cinema. Cramming a toffee in her mouth, she crumpled the wrapper and threw it at her feet. The dogs jumped. The little girl screamed and scuttled off, and the dogs barked, and another passer-by, enraged at their behaviour, jabbed his umbrella towards them like it was a sword.

No! I said. And I started to say even more, none of it polite, but I stopped myself.

What did I know of these people's relationship with the dogs? For all I knew the dogs had rabies and had given many of the people rabies too.

So while the man yelled and the dogs barked, I stood with a bag of puffed rice in my hand and hoped the matter would resolve itself.

When Ramesh arrived, I raised my voice and said, I'm leaving now, namaste, hoping that the man would be on his way as well. I jumped into the jeep, but I couldn't resist another look. The dogs were up and running. But they weren't running away from the man. They were chasing after me.

We drove the only way the driver knew how to drive, but we were still too late. In the village the boy's mother sat outside her hut, hair undone, sari carelessly bundled around her thick waist. She picked at her teeth and threw blame wherever it might stick.

It was his friends' fault; they taunted him about his clothes. It was the neighbour; she asked how he dared act *dabang*, tough, when he wasn't even tough enough to keep a job. It was an uncle from the village across the pond; he gave the boy a thousand rupees and a sack of rice. Now the boy's mother had money and food, but not her son.

The boy from the cowshed was gone.

The village across the pond was occupied by upper-caste families. They lived in brick houses and owned the fields on which the lower-caste families of Amni worked, not even for cash, but for a few sacks of grain a year. The lower-caste families never walked over to the other side, not unless they had a very good reason, and the upper-caste men only came around when they wanted to hire labour. The villagers were neighbours, but their lives were worlds apart.

'They took my son,' cried the boy's mother.

The militias could no longer be blamed. They had been wiped out years earlier. The death of Brahmeshwar Nath Singh, leader of the Ranvir Sena, formed the epilogue. He had been gunned down in the summer of 2012 while out on his morning walk. Bihar even had a new, progressive and some said brilliant chief minister. Nitish Kumar had brought electricity to some villages, and designated certain Dalit communities as Maha Dalit, underscoring their extreme vulnerability. Even the Naxalites had moved on, they were now a nationwide group determined to overthrow the Indian government.

Change *had* come, just not to Amni.

Into this void stepped two men, daily wage labourers, like all the other men in Amni. They had some education, which was rare in these parts, and they worked for a local non-profit – this was the only explanation for their unusual behaviour.

They saw child trafficking and child labour for what it was, and in doing so marked themselves as different from the other villagers.

When a child disappeared, the men used their sources to find out where he was. They gathered the villagers and collected funds to go there. They'd stopped approaching the police – always bored and dismissive – a long time ago. The men had been to Delhi and Haryana and Varanasi, and countless dusty, crowded industrial towns on their quest, and in each place they did the same thing. They gathered a crowd and held placards, raising slogans against child labour. They stood in the sun for as many hours as it took for the factory gates to open and someone to come out. The factory managers always tried to argue their way out of handing over the child for free. 'I paid for him,' they said. 'He's mine.' But soon enough, unwilling to attract attention over one easily replaceable worker, they would shove him out.

There are happy endings to such stories, but so far the men had experienced none.

'We return to fanfare,' said one of them. 'But soon everyone turns on us. They ask what we expect them to eat. They swear never to help us again.'

The boy from the cowshed had been rescued twice before. And the men wanted to rescue him again. In a few hours they would start a collection. They had already approached the boy's mother. She had asked them to come back the next day. They spoke to her husband as well, but he was in no position to contribute money.

'This is what I do,' said the man. 'Bring back children, even children no one wants back.'

The village elder who had told us of the Best Hotel told us other things as well. The day we met the boy and the boy took us to his mother, the old man came along and sat outside their hut on a rope bed.

'The children sell themselves,' he said.

The boy nodded.

'The children call them Uncle, Auntie, but they don't know them at all. A few are upper castes. They cross the pond looking for servants, *darzis*, coal miners, whatever they want. And barely have they walked back than the children race up to them begging, take me, choose me, I want to go!' He hacked and spat. 'It's big business. And for people who reach into their pockets only to touch air, it's good business. You call them . . . What do you call them? *Hahn*, traffickers. They say, "We're businessmen." '

'Boys.' The boy's mother shrugged. 'They never listen to their parents.'

The boy reared his head. 'If I don't go, what will we eat?'

'My son's father is a good-for-nothing,' his mother said. 'And I'm only a woman. But ask anyone – I didn't sell my son like some third-class person. If he went, it was because he wanted to.'

'Who will stop me?' asked her child. He wasn't demanding to know; he was curious, perhaps even hopeful that someone would stop him from leaving, stop him from working fourteen-hour days. He leaned his bony back against the mud wall, tipped his face and drew his knees to his chin with a sigh. Soon he would get bored with his mother's complaints ('The well is filthy; if not of hunger, surely we will die of cholera!') and slink out of the hut. At dusk when I left Amni, I saw him seated around a small fire in front of the tea shop. playing cards with men twice his age. He was laughing and his eyes shone in the light of the flames.

When would he go home? I wondered. When the fire died?

But the village had no electricity, and some fires blazed all night.

I had found the smell. There was a small plastic dustbin next to the television, and when I pressed the pedal with my foot the lid jumped up to reveal a substance filled to the brim. It was the colour of dried blood. As I was leaving, I complained to the man at the reception. I said, the dustbin in my room is full of spit. Your guests have been spitting tobacco into it.

'What can I do?' he asked plaintively.

You could clean it, I replied.

'Madam,' he said, 'what is the point of cleaning something that only gets dirty again?' ∎

Geese

there is no cure for temperament it's how
we recognize ourselves but sometimes within it
a narrowing imprisons or is opened such as when my mother
in her last illness snarled and spat and how this lifted my dour father
into a patient tenderness thereby astounding everyone
but mostly it hardens who we always were

if you've been let's say a glass-half-empty kind of girl
you wake to the chorus of geese overhead
forlorn for something has softened their nasal voices
their ugly aggression on the ground they're worse than chickens
but flying one leader falling back another moving up to pierce the wind
no one in charge or every one in charge in flight each limited goose
adjusts its part in the cluster just under the clouds
do they mean together to duplicate the cloud
like the pelicans on the pond rearranging their shadows
to fool the fish another collective that constantly recalibrates but fish
don't need to reinvent themselves the way geese do
when they negotiate the sky
                              on the fixed
unyielding ground there is no end to hierarchy
the flock the pack the family you know it's true if you're
a take-charge kind of girl I recommend

house plants in the windows facing south
the cacti the cyclamen are blooming on the brink
of winter all it took was a little enforced deprivation
a little premature and structured dark

BLOOD MONEY

Miroslav Penkov

At first the Gypsies didn't know how to answer their cellphone. Toshev had sent it to them in a box with written instructions, but every time he called, the phone went straight to voicemail. 'Gypsies can't read,' his editor told him. 'No disrespect to you, my boy, but that's a fact. And one more fact – the cost of the phone comes out of your pocket.'

Toshev knew all that, of course. But with this story, he was hoping for a change. He had saved up enough money for bribes and had already reserved the Sony camcorder and the Zenith camera from the copy room. So he telegraphed the village postman and promised him ten euros if he could get the Gypsies to answer. An hour later he reached voicemail again. At his desk he pretended to work on the article, but his thoughts were a fishing seine that wrapped around him tighter the more he struggled. He needed to take pictures of the woman, ask her questions and videotape her answers. This was all he knew with some clarity.

Behind his back his colleagues were already making fun of him. 'Would you look at Toshev,' someone said in passing, 'killing that story.'

'*He* should know better,' someone else said.

So, to ignore them, Toshev typed a line of commas and full stops. Then he typed: *My thanks to the committee, for giving me this esteemed journalistic award. Award*, he retyped. *Award me.*

An hour later he dialled again and waited while the line sank silent and crackled. At last he heard a woman's voice.

'It's me,' he said and sprang to his feet. His knees caught the desk and a stack of papers scattered to the floor. His mug spilled out a mix of old coffee grounds and sugar sludge. 'Can we talk? Are you good to talk?'

'We good,' said the woman.

Toshev ran out into the hallway. He flew up the stairs and kicked open the door to the roof. He didn't bother to make sure the door wouldn't lock behind him. He was too busy setting his phone to record. 'Essil,' he said. 'Are you still there?'

'Been here for forty years,' the woman said and in the background Toshev picked up muffled voices, the slam of a door or a window and wind blowing. 'Ahmed,' she yelled. 'God damn you, boy . . . the plague take you,' or so Toshev imagined. It had been years since he had last heard someone speak Romani. 'Ma'am,' he said in Bulgarian, trying to steady his breathing, 'my clients . . . Missus Papadopoulos, she wants to see pictures of you. She wants me to come up there and film you for a few minutes.'

The woman asked him to repeat what he had just said over the wind howling on the other side and so he repeated it.

'You listen to me,' she told him. 'There's nothing to film here. You tell those Greeks we're healthy folk. You tell them how high it's sitting. It'll be a boy.'

'Essil,' he cut her off. He knew she would only get herself worked up if he let her speak and he didn't want her to feel empowered. That's how he'd rationalized it, lying in bed at night, thinking. Never let her feel empowered. She's a horse, and you're its master. Hold the reins tight. Also, he couldn't afford a lengthy phone call. So now, when he spoke again, his voice was surprisingly even. 'My clients need pictures or there will be no deal. They want to see film of you. No film, Essil, means no deal,' he said, and leaned on the ledge.

Down on the street, a current of cars and buses flowed black with exhaust, and in the distance Mount Vitosha stood barely visible through the February fog.

'All right,' the woman said at last. 'But pictures will be a thousand euro more. Five thousand total. For pictures and the baby.'

Toshev pretended to consider something.

'I'll be coming on the night train,' he said.

Half a year ago Toshev had been assigned a minor corruption case. Some lawyer had paid the prosecution to get his client off the hook and Toshev gathered enough dirt for a fine story. Desperate, the lawyer had offered to give Toshev information about an international scheme that would make a much finer piece, and Toshev, in turn desperate for recognition, had agreed to close his eyes and to listen.

It was getting dark by the time he reached the train station. In his wagon he found an empty compartment and took the seat farthest from the door, under the window. He rubbed his hands together, blew a ball of warm air into them and pulled the bag he was carrying closer. He checked it again. The Zenith and the Sony camcorder were in there, so he threw the strap across his chest and huddled tight in his jacket.

For years, the lawyer had said, the countries of the Eastern bloc had been making money selling orphans to foreign adopters. Even a child in poor health or with mental deficiencies could cost as much as 80,000 dollars. And now Bulgaria was in the EU, which meant that travel and trade were easier. The scheme was simple. A Gypsy woman was paid to carry a child, then a week before her due date, she was secretly transported, let's say to Greece, where she gave birth in a hospital. The adoptive couple paid her three or four thousand euros, kept the child and sent her back to Bulgaria.

Toshev knew that it would be pointless to go after the lawyers in the scheme, with all their connections, or after the foreign adopters, with all their money. So he decided to seek a more human angle to the story. He pressured his informant until at last he received the name of a woman, in a village on the Danube, who was willing to sell her child. He reached the woman through a third person and presented himself as the attorney of a childless couple from Greece. The Gypsy had little interest in the details. 'Four thousand euro,' she told him. 'That's what we want.'

The train began to move. The windows buzzed in their rusty frames and the vibrations in the floor spread through Toshev, heels to teeth. Out in the gloom, on the platform, he could glimpse people seeing someone off, waving briefly, then hurrying to hide their hands back in their pockets. He wondered how it would feel if there was one person on this platform to see him off. Good, he thought. It would feel good.

For days after he had first spoken with the woman, Toshev could not sleep. He told himself that his interest in the story was purely professional. That if written the right way this report would surely fetch him an award. His salary would increase and he would finally be able to rent a whole apartment, not just an attic above the room of a cello player. But his interest, he knew all along, was not professional at all.

The door to the compartment slid open and in the glass he saw that a woman had entered. The air was suddenly thick with the musk of her perfume. She was young and pretty and Toshev turned from the window to greet her.

The woman was pulling a magazine out of her handbag when he wished her a good evening.

'It's a bitter night, isn't it?' he said and for the first time the woman looked up and saw him. She glanced at his face very quickly, then at his shoes, bag, face again.

Then she shoved the magazine in her handbag. 'Wrong compartment,' she mumbled, stood up and hurried away. For an instant, Toshev thought of chasing her down, of telling her, don't worry, please sit beside me, read your magazine safely. He was an educated man. He had written for magazines like hers. But just as quickly an acid hatred climbed up his oesophagus and he knew that if she were to come back again he would slap her, with the back of his hand: a good, old-fashioned Gypsy slap. So, with the window open, he stood against the whips of cold and waited for her cheap perfume to leak out into the night.

Toshev's own mother had given him up for adoption just a few days after his birth, and he had lived in an orphanage, unchosen, for eighteen years. His nickname had been *Majo*, from *majun*, or putty, because as a five-year-old another boy had told him the putty on the sink pipes was gum. Toshev had glued his jaws together and the name had stuck. But that nickname, he knew, could have very well addressed the colour of his skin. Of all the orphans, he had been the darkest. As a little boy he imagined his mother beautiful and white, almost transparent, with blue eyes and lush, blonde hair. He spoke to the other children with contempt, called them gyppos, spat at their chests. 'My mother was beautiful and white,' he told them, 'but my father was a gyppo like you, darker than soot. So he raped her and that's how I was born.' The other children envied him for this. They beat him, threw stones at him, left him with embittering little scars; and, in his mind, each new scar etched his white mother a little more clearly.

At six, he broke into the director's office, hoping to find a photograph that showed his mother's blue eyes and straw hair, or perhaps an address in a good part of Sofia he could use to locate her once he ran away. But inside the office he found only a single leaflet in his folder which, judging by the names on the cover – each crossed out with a different pen – had once belonged to four other boys. In the folder was his birth certificate, with his mother's name – a Gypsy name – and a date for his birth different from the one he'd been told by a whole month.

That night he had narrated his usual story to the few kids always eager to beat him up. His mother had been walking her toy poodle in the dark, when his father jumped at her from around a corner. But when he was done with the telling, for the first time in many years no one knuckled his head, no one held him by his wrists to spin him violently around and then let go so his body would go crashing into a wall, a chair, a table. They knew that he knew, and they had probably known all along. After that night, he never spoke of his white mother again.

At eighteen, he left the orphanage with fifty levs in his pocket, money he stole from a teacher. He no longer felt the need to find out who his mother was. He did not bother imagining her possible lives; he was not concerned with any possible family or other children she might have.

And then the woman on the Danube had demanded four thousand euros for her baby, and something had woken up in Toshev – some curiosity or hatred, he couldn't tell – and for the first time in many years he had thought of her.

The whistle shrieked and the sound bounced off the station; the train moved on. He was left alone on the empty platform. Not a soul. A wide spot on the facade of the station building, where water had leaked and frozen, now shone like a giant mirror before him. The rest was snow. As far as he could see – a flat white field under a white morning sky. And wind. With nothing to stop it, the wind had scoured the snow into a polished crust. Toshev couldn't see the Danube, but in the distance he recognized the smoke of chimneys. He started trudging through the snow – knee-deep below the crust in places – and by the time he reached the village, he was shaking from the cold.

In the tavern he drank tea, and asked about the encampment. The shacks were beyond the last village house, close to the levee, the tavern keeper told him, wetting a towel and cleaning a glass. For some time he watched Toshev without a word. Then he said, 'In a perfect world, we would have dumped them in the river.'

Of course Toshev knew the man was trying to pick a fight. He'd fought plenty such fights in the years after the orphanage, at the university, in the cafeteria at work, waiting in line for the city bus. But he was too cold for a fight now.

'In a perfect world,' he said, 'the winters would be milder, my pockets full of cash. And I'd be anywhere but here.'

The man shivered as though, suddenly, he too had lost his fighting desire to the cold. 'I'll drink to that,' he said, and poured some *mastika* in Toshev's tea.

On his way out, Toshev left an envelope with the ten euros he'd promised the postman. He walked through empty streets, with houses whose chimneys smoked with thick, black puffs. The wind caught the smoke before it had risen and hurled it down with such force that the snow on both sides of the path was black and shiny with soot.

Beyond the last house were more fields and then the levee – a wave of frozen earth across the horizon, white as bone, but for the charcoal patches where wind had swept the snow away. It seemed to Toshev he had reached the edge of a flat world, and that the levee was there to stop him from falling off into the nothing. He grew fearful of the Gypsies. He thought he could smell their sour sweat, their rotten breath above the wind. In his head, he heard their dirty rambling, stuttering and cursing – the language he hadn't spoken in more than a decade.

He was near the shacks now, when suddenly the white before him jumped up with squawks and a flap of feathers. Without noticing, he'd walked into a flock of geese, as pale as the snow and huddled against the cold. The geese hissed at him, necks extended, beaks clacking. With each wing-flap rose a gust of air so sharp it slashed his face. Each wing-flap brought them closer, so close he could feel the heat their bodies spilled.

'Git, git, you brutes,' he heard a voice say and at once he was saved. A boy, not ten feet away, snuck alongside a goose and stroked it, and then snapped its neck and flung it over his shoulder. 'We'll tell the farmers you scared her off to the river,' the boy said and his big eyes shone black like the soot. His skin was almost as dark as Toshev's.

'I'm looking for Essil, the pregnant woman.'

A sly smile stretched the boy's lips and Toshev reached for his wallet even before the boy had spoken: 'One lev and I will take you to her shack.'

He paid the boy and followed. In his accented Bulgarian, the boy asked him where he came from, if he supported CSKA or Levski, and if the trams in Sofia were as noisy as his cousin had once told him they were. Then the boy switched to Romani.

'How come you're so dark?'

Toshev pretended he did not understand. The old anger rose up and choked him. He heard the voice of children from the orphanage and for a moment the earth spun before his eyes.

'Speak in Bulgarian,' he said to the boy and then some other feeling – regret or maybe shame – pushed the anger away. Quiet, he watched the dead goose flop against the boy's back as they trudged through the snow.

Tin sheets formed the shacks, which were covered with rugs, wood and cardboard to stop the wind. Outside, children played with a pack of dogs. Their feet were wrapped in rags and scraps of plastic packaging. They had churned the snow into slush. Toshev saw old men fixing a roof that had collapsed, and women stirring pots over tiny fires. He tasted the bitter smoke. All eyes were on him as he followed the boy.

The door was a wooden plank, swollen with rot in the corners. The boy called out to someone, then went to the side of the shack and began to pluck the goose, not even bothering to scald it first. He dropped feathers at his feet in large frozen clumps and called again. The door moved, Toshev heard cursing and a girl stood outside, her stomach large under her coat and a shotgun in her hands.

'Ahmed, you fool,' she said to the boy in Romani. 'He could be one of those killers.'

'He's no killer. He is the lawyer from the city.'

The girl looked at Toshev. Like the woman on the train her eyes slid from his face to his shoes and up again. '*Maman*,' she called, slightly turning to the gaping door, but still holding Toshev in her aim. '*Maman*, the lawyer is here.'

An American woman had made an attempt to adopt Toshev when he was seven years old. Or so it had seemed. A teacher had roused him from his afternoon nap, and he'd staggered between the rows of bunk beds, knowing the other children were watching him, knowing he would not escape the beating upon his return. It was raining that afternoon and the teacher – most likely to appear benevolent before the foreigner – let him hold his own umbrella as they splashed through the muddy puddles in the yard. At the gates, a red car waited for him, the reddest car he'd ever seen or would see, with the rain and the sky so dark, so close to the ground. The car was not a Moskvich, not a Lada. He did not recognize the emblem, but remembered it, and for years after that emblem was all he drew in the dust of the orphanage's desks, tables and cupboards.

There was a woman in the back seat, a very blonde woman, who held the door open. She said something he did not understand and motioned for him to get in. He tried to close his umbrella, but couldn't. The rain pelted down while he wrestled with the spikes, a deluge so noisy it muffled the woman's laughter.

The teacher yanked the umbrella from his hands and shoved him in the car.

'Don't fuck this up,' she told him before leaving.

He sat stiffly in the back seat, hands on his thighs, afraid to move, rainwater trickling down his back, itchy. The woman said something. Something funny, because the driver – there was a driver of course, a man with a thick neck and hair shorn as close to the skin as Toshev's – laughed. So Toshev, too, started laughing. The woman laid a hand on his knee, and the hand burned him, that's how warm it was, with its fingers long and thin, and nails painted red like the car. If he hadn't already seen his file in the principal's office Toshev would have believed this really was his imaginary mother coming to take him away. But even having seen the file, he thought that, and wished it all through their afternoon together. They took him to Sofia, to a sweet shop. The driver waited in the car, while in the cafe the woman ordered *garash* cake and lemonade and *boza* for him. She sat across the tiny table, ate nothing, drank nothing, but watched him and smiled. Every now and then she said something unintelligible, yet so funny in its sound Toshev could do nothing but laugh through the mouthfuls of chocolate.

'What kinda car is that, comrade?' he kept asking and the woman must have thought he wanted more cake because she kept sending the waiter to fetch it.

On the way back, he fell asleep in her arms. He had a nice dream, but when the car door finally opened he was startled, did not know where he was right away and began crying.

Outside, in the rain, the teacher waited, this time with no umbrella for him.

The woman held him tightly. She smelled like nothing he'd ever smelled before, a scent so novel it frightened and consoled him in equal measure. Like a leech, he latched onto this smell and tried to drink it. The woman peeled him off at last. She brushed the tears off his cheeks and patted his stomach, which had started to rumble from the cake.

He watched the car drive off in the dark, its brake lights like little red stars before it disappeared around the corner. He would never see the woman again; would never find out why she'd given up on the adoption. He tried to tell himself it hadn't been his fault and yet, for many years afterwards, mostly at night when it was much too dark for sleep, her smell returned to him like sweet, blonde laughter. Don't fuck this up, the laughter sometimes told him.

So it was not Essil, but her daughter who was pregnant. A girl who to Toshev looked no older than sixteen. A girl who, he realized, would make his story stronger.

'That's a piddling matter,' the woman said grandly, leading him into the shack, clearly assured that her daughter's pregnancy was too far advanced now for the deal to be off. So that's why they had been reluctant to let him visit them and film. Toshev wondered how long they had expected to keep up with the charade.

They sat him down on the only chair, close to the stove. He turned his tape recorder on and held his bag tight. Rugs covered the floor; some were wet while others were frozen solid. Wind blew through cracks in the ceiling, cracks where the walls joined. The woman, Essil, and the girl sat across from him, on a large bed, the shotgun propped between them.

'The money,' Toshev said in Bulgarian, because money was the first thing Essil had asked to see. They'd get the rest once the baby was born. For now, he said, this should suffice. He counted off a hundred levs, the last of his savings. The woman took the bills and tucked them in her shirt. Her frame was bony, her face was wrinkled and the teeth in her mouth were few. She was cross-eyed and she never seemed to look straight at him. And so he relaxed, amending the lies he had rehearsed with ease.

A car would come the week before the baby was due to pick up the girl and drive her down to Greece. Got your ID ready? Good. We'll take you to a little town close to the border, a town with a nice hospital. You'll have the baby there, with doctors and nurses, and the best equipment. The Papadopouloses are very concerned with the safety and health of their child. We'll keep you in the hospital a few more days. We'll pay you – five thousand euros – and then the car will drive you home.

The girl's eyes were on him as he spoke. Every now and then he caught glimpses of her stomach under the coat, and of her hands, which she cradled in her lap like dead fish. Her back was straight and she barely breathed.

'I need to take some photos now,' he said and pulled the Zenith out of the bag.

'Your eye is twitching,' the mother said and asked him what date he was born. 'An even month,' she said when he told her. 'And it's your left eye twitching. That's a good sign. Something good will happen.'

He mumbled words even he himself did not understand. Then, while they sat on the bed, he took their pictures, pictures of the stove, the bed, the ceiling. 'Can we get the boy in?'

They called the boy.

'A storm's coming,' the boy said from the threshold and stomped his feet to shake off the snow. Essil wrestled with the door to close it tightly before the wind could blow more snow inside. In the distance, Toshev caught a glimpse of the sky, no longer white, but the colour of damp ash.

He positioned the boy between the two women and told them to hold their pose. The boy's hands were bloody from the goose and feathers stuck to the blood, which made for a fine picture. Then

Toshev set the camcorder on the tripod but at first it wouldn't start for the cold.

'So,' Toshev said at last, watching the girl in the camera screen. He asked for her name.

'Sofi,' the girl said and he asked how old she was.

'Going on thirteen.'

So she was twelve, he said.

'Going on thirteen.'

'And you're pregnant.'

The girl raised an eyebrow.

Then he asked if she lived here with her mother, with her little brother.

'That's all that's left.'

'Meaning?'

'Everyone else, Grandpa, my father, my brothers, are all dead now.'

Her mother stirred. 'Listen, mister lawyer,' she said in her broken Bulgarian, trying to look straight into the camera lens. Her words came out with difficulty, like the words of the girl. 'Don't ask Sofi such things. Don't make us look bad. We aren't violent people. We are gentle folk with talent. Sofi, sing "Ederlezi" for the Greeks.'

At once the girl began singing. Her voice was clean and ringing like laughter, mighty inside the tiny shack. Her brother got up and clapped and stomped his feet, snapped his fingers and danced in a flutter of bloody, thawing feathers.

All this surprised Toshev. He remembered girls at the orphanage singing this same song, and the teachers beating them if they heard it, making them sing 'Tall, Blue Mountains' or 'Fatherland, How Beautiful You Are' or other proper Bulgarian songs.

'Sofi,' he said. He looked up from the camera. Her eyes were small, and they glistened like a fox's that watched him unblinkingly. 'Why are you selling your baby?'

She rubbed a thumb and an index finger together.

'Are there no jobs?' he asked, and she told him there were no jobs.

A warm, prickly wave of blood washed through his body, all the way to the tips of his fingers. No jobs, no money, life is hard for a Gypsy. He'd heard it all before, the usual drivel; he'd let that drivel roll off his own tongue before.

'Sofi, Sofi,' he said. He hoped that repeating her name would calm him a little. It did. But now he realized he was cold again. 'I'm cold,' he said suddenly, almost surprised at his own words. 'Can I get some hot water, some tea?'

'Tea?' Essil sneered. 'Tea rusts the gut. I'll do you one better. Ahmed,' she called, 'bring the kettle.'

With a joyful yap, the boy sprang off the bed and sank to his knees in the corner. He hesitated for a moment, looked back at his mother, and only after she'd given him permission again did he peel off a rug from the floor; half frozen, the rug remained rolled at one end, like the front of a toboggan, and there under the rug was a wooden hatch which the boy threw open. He lay flat by the gaping hole in the floor, stuck his head in, rummaged, then pulled out, one by one, a wooden mortar, a rusty green kettle and a wicker demijohn, its mouth corked up with a corncob wrapped in a pink cloth.

Toshev kept filming as the boy passed the demijohn to his mother with reverence as if it were a round loaf for the blessing. They filled up the kettle and the sharp smell of liquor sloshed through the shed. The boy sniffed at the spout and his eyes watered; then he carried the kettle to the stove and, with the same reverence, set it upon the hotplate.

'Plum *rakia*,' the boy said without turning. 'Older than I am.' Then he stood by the stove, waiting for the liquor to heat up properly.

Toshev had no desire to drink with the Gypsies. He wanted to ask some more questions, get the answers on tape, bid everyone farewell and make it to the train before sunset. He looked up at Essil, who showed him her gums. 'You tell the Greeks we're nice people. You tell them you were cold and we wined you, hungry and we dined you.' The kettle sizzled. The boy hid his hand in his sleeve, caught the handle and filled the wooden mortar with steaming *rakia*. He brought the mortar to Toshev and held it before him, with two hands. Toshev took it and drank. The *rakia* was stronger than he'd expected. He gasped, but the fumes choked him. Sofi laughed and the boy shook his head. He turned to his mother and when she waved benevolently he took the mortar from Toshev and drank. 'Brother in heaven,' the boy said, 'she kicks like a catfish.'

Toshev laughed against his will. He had misunderstood the boy, or the boy had strung together the wrong words, and in a passing instant these words had sounded funny. The boy too was laughing. He allowed Toshev one more gulp before he drank the mortar dry.

'Listen,' Toshev said. He looked at the camcorder, taping, then at Essil and her daughter. They were both smiling and so was the boy, who'd gone back to the kettle and was refilling the mortar. Toshev looked at the girl's stomach. 'Listen,' he repeated, but did not know what exactly it was he wanted to say. All he could think of was the baby, and for the first time, or so it seemed, he recognized that there were no Greek buyers, no Greek money, that he had made everything up. He wondered what the girl would do with the baby once it was born. But these thoughts rushed through his head, without time for him to consider them in so many words. All they left was a metallic taste on his palate, a heaviness in his stomach, which he took not for anger at himself because of what he was doing, but at the women because of what they were about to do. A powerful gust slapped the walls of the shed, and the walls shivered and closed down on him. Panting, Toshev sprang up to his feet, ready to pack.

'Thank you,' he muttered. They had been very helpful, but he had a train to catch.

'Come on, mister lawyer,' Essil said. 'Stay for lunch.'

At the door he promised to call again once the due date was closer and he reminded them to keep the phone on. Then he wondered if they even had electricity to charge its battery. But he didn't want to spend more time asking or explaining things. Outside, the goose was boiling in a deep, blackened cauldron, yet everything smelled not of food, but of chimneys. The village shacks were lined up in such a way that they formed tunnels through which, sped up, the wind dragged smoke in thick ropes. The gusts shaved off frost from the crusty ground and turned it up in the air in fistfuls, which in turn caught and tossed about pieces of cardboard, nylon bags, other garbage. There were no more children playing outside, no more dogs, and as he bid the Gypsies goodbye, as he refused the boy's offer to guide him out of the village, Toshev wondered, briefly, whether he should not just stay inside and wait the storm out.

And so, once he was out of the village, his desire to see the river was even stranger to him. But he needed to see it, to climb up on the levee where the air was cleaner, where all the soot, and dirt, and smell would no longer crush him.

The wind was stronger up on the levee, more vicious. Down below, at his feet, was the Danube, wide and grey, and so sluggish he couldn't even see it moving. Along the Bulgarian bank he saw boats, flipped over so as not to gather snow, with their blue bellies up in the air, and piles of fishing seines black on the shore. Two large ships stood upriver, and several smaller boats clustered about them, and Toshev thought of the Sofia buses and cars nuzzling up against one another. And beyond these was the Romanian bank, a thick bare forest.

He was very cold now. His head hurt and felt misty from the *rakia* he'd drunk on an empty stomach. He was hungry. He was still angry. He took some pictures of the river and the ships and the sky growing blacker above the Bulgarian side. He knew he had to go back down and make for the train as quickly as possible, and yet he could not move. Watching the Danube, he realized that, most likely even before he'd bid the Gypsies goodbye, he had already made up his mind to return to their shack and eat their lunch. And then he understood that the Danube was frozen, its waves grey ice from one bank to the other, west to east, all the way to the Black Sea. He watched it, atop the levee, until his face went numb.

He swallowed whole chunks of the goose without chewing much. The meat burned his mouth. The *rakia* blazed down his throat and he felt the sweat budding out on his back and forehead. They were sitting on the floor, around the steaming carcass, and no one was speaking; only the boy grunted and mumbled to let everyone know just how tasty he thought the dish was. Outside the wind had got unbearable, and the walls of the shack shivered with its gusts. Wood cracked in the stove and light escaped through the little peephole in its lid and flickered orange on the trembling ceiling.

Opposite Toshev, the girl kept her hands stiff in her lap, and a few times he caught her looking at him, then hurrying to look away, with flushed cheeks. She barely touched the food, but still her lips glistened from the fat, and in the gloom of the shack her pupils seemed very large. She looked pretty, or so Toshev thought, and so he kept his eyes on the goose.

Essil had been pleased to see him at their threshold again.

'You did smart to come back,' she'd said, and wrestled the door shut behind him. She'd ordered the boy to fill up the kettle, while Sofi had offered him her seat by the stove.

And now, he was eating much the same way he'd eaten in the orphanage, when food had been scarce and you had to gobble or go to bed hungry. Only now, there was plenty of goose before him, and he did not understand why, after all these years, he was acting in the same old, ugly way. His eyes fell on the shotgun, propped against the bed behind Sofi, and this time to chase the silence away he spoke: 'What's with the shotgun?'

The boy held out his hand and Toshev passed him the mortar. Essil did not protest when the boy drank. 'For protection,' the boy said and it was then that Essil protested.

'Listen,' she said. 'Don't tell the Greeks about the shotgun. We're not bad people.'

Why do you care what I tell the Greeks? Toshev wanted to ask. Why do you care if they think you good people or bad?

'It's for the Wallachians,' Sofi said quickly, before her mother could stop her. The mother narrowed her lazy eyes. *Keep quiet*, she said in Romani, but in Bulgarian Toshev asked her to please let the girl finish.

Essil reached for the mortar and told the boy to fill it up again. She took a thirsty gulp and wiped her lips with a tress of her hair. When she tried to look up at Toshev, her eyes were burning, and her lips were stretched in a smile, but pressed tightly, hiding the gaps from her missing teeth. The oily lock of hair shone like a curved silver blade.

'Two years ago,' she said, 'these men came to our shack. Five of them, tall, big, bearded men, *vlasi*, Wallachians from across the Danube, from Romania. I was sitting right here by this stove when they called out. "Kara Oglu home?" Kara Oglu was these kids' grandpa. "Kara Oglu's fishing," I told them. "You care to sit down and wait?" "We waited fifty years," the men said. "We can wait another hour." And they sat outside by the cooking fire and waited. Finally our men came home – my big boys and little Ahmed here, and my husband and Grandpa. They meet the Wallachians outside and the Wallachians ask Grandpa, "Kara Oglu, do you remember Hanash Begner?" Grandpa turns all pale and stutters, "I don't remember Hanash Begner." "Kara Oglu," the Wallachians say, "fifty years ago, after the big war, when you were across the river, you murdered Hanash Begner and stole from him four hundred bank bonds and a silver case for tobacco. We are his kin and we've come to seek blood, Kara Oglu, from you and from your kin." And the men take out knives and cut their palms and let blood on the ground. "This, Kara Oglu, is a blood feud," they say, "and it won't be over until your male kin is buried." And the men turn to leave us, but my biggest boy, he goes inside and grabs the shotgun and he shoots one of the Wallachians in the head. He had to shoot him, you see.'

'Two months later,' Sofi said and broke off a wing from the goose, 'the Wallachians got Grandpa by the river. Then each week after, they got another of our boys. Now it's this boy here – Ahmed – who's left, and as soon as he turns eleven they'll come to shoot him too.' She sank her teeth into the wing and sucked on its juice.

'I'd like to see them try,' Ahmed said, his speech a little slurred.

When he reached for the mortar, his mother slapped his hand.

'So we got two choices,' she said. 'Kill the Wallachians, which we can't, or pay them the blood money to end the feud.'

'The blood money,' Toshev repeated.

'Four thousand euro,' Essil said. 'That's why we're selling.'

Toshev asked the boy to fill up the mortar.

'I'm fine sitting for now,' the boy grinned. Toshev asked for their permission and got up and brought the kettle from the stove. He poured himself more *rakia* and drank.

'So Kara Oglu,' he asked, 'did he really kill the *vlah*?'

'Killed him with a dagger,' the girl said and smiled wide.

'And what happens if you don't pay them the four thousand?'

Essil tensed up. 'Why wouldn't we?' she said.

'Hypothetically, what happens?'

'Well,' she said, 'in March, Ahmed turns eleven.'

'And so, you're selling.'

'We heard about this deal from a neighbour. I would have got a baby if I could. But then Sofi here is old enough.'

'She is twelve years old,' Toshev said.

'Listen, mister lawyer,' the boy said, 'if eleven is old enough to get shot . . .' but the boy didn't finish.

'And the father? The Papadopouloses specifically told me to ask about the father.'

'I chose the father,' Essil said. 'He is a good boy. I brought him here myself and waited for him to do it. He got the job done the first time.'

'You want to know what he looks like?' Sofi asked and raised an eyebrow. 'He's fine. Two rows of good teeth, very elegant. And he doesn't stutter.'

'Oh yes, he stutters,' the boy said and burst out laughing.

Not knowing why, Toshev too began to laugh. It was not funny at all, the way the girl stuck her lower lip out, the way her cheeks blushed again, the way she turned her hands into fists. None of this was funny to Toshev, and yet he kept on laughing.

'I got a question,' Sofi spoke when the laughter subsided, 'about those Greeks.'

'What's the question?'

'Are they rich?'

'Rich, very rich,' he lied.

'I want my kid to grow up rich. Like you maybe, a lawyer. I want him to have his own room, and a bathroom with a tub . . .'

But Toshev could not afford to listen any longer. Instead he poured himself more *rakia* and listened to the howling wind outside, and to the logs bursting with heat in the iron belly of the stove, and tried to imagine the flames burning the wood and reducing it to cold, grey ash. He remembered the grey ice of the Danube, and the barren forest on the Romanian bank, where the Wallachians lived. Big, tall, hairy men, who'd come to avenge their own, goaded on by blood, blood alive and foaming in their veins, blood like rope, which tied one Wallachian to another, so that one would not know peace while another was restless. Blood, this blood rose around him now and he drank it boiling from the mortar, and it made him dizzy, and he watched the girl smile at him, with her lips glowing and her belly swollen with life.

'Sing,' he said in Romani. The word rolled off his tongue with ease, the word itself a tiny song. 'Sing "Ederlezi". I want to hear it.' For some time they watched him, surprised. So he closed his eyes and when the girl began singing, he swayed with her voice. Her mother joined in, and then the boy. At once, the air filled up with mould, with the smell of boiled cabbage, with the stench of bleach. The girls of the orphanage were singing before him, holding their hands and singing.

All the Roma, Mama, are slaughtering lambs today.
But poor me, I'm sitting apart.
It's Ederlezi, Mama. St George's feast.

And then he felt Sofi's face on his shoulder, and those same lips of hers on his neck and on his own.

With a yell he sprang up, stumbled and hurled the mortar at the wall. In Romani he called the girl a whore, and her mother he called worse things. He was half aware that the boy had snatched the shotgun and was holding him in his aim, and that the shotgun shook in the boy's small hands. He was half aware that the girl and her mother had embraced his knees and now kissed the knuckles of his hands and begged him for forgiveness.

'Forgive us,' they cried and asked him to return to them, back to the floor, by the stove, where they'd be warm together. And so he sat down, and so the boy put down the shotgun and poured him more *rakia* and so they drank together, down on the floor, by the stove, where they were warm.

Toshev awoke on the floor with his temples splitting and his lips coated with congealed fat. He was thirstier than he'd ever been, and for a moment, as happened sometimes when he awoke startled, he didn't know where he was exactly. The wind still howled outside and rattled the tin walls, but the fire had died down in the stove and light no longer moved along the ceiling. It was completely dark in the shack, like the inside of a coiled ram's horn.

Then he understood that something heavy lay on his chest and constricted his breathing. He grew frightened, on the verge of panic, because he couldn't breathe, no matter how much he struggled. But whatever lay on his chest stirred, and someone's warm breath hit his face with the smell of *rakia*. Or maybe it was his own breath that bounced off the face in the dark. He wasn't certain.

'These Greeks,' a voice said, above the snoring that came from the bed. 'Are they truly rich?'

He wanted to push the girl away, but instead, he closed his eyes and opened them, which made no difference. He tried to swallow, but his throat spasmed, and a bursting pulse rushed through his temples. He understood that he was still drunk.

'Yes,' he said, 'the Greeks are very wealthy.'

'So my boy, he will speak Greek, won't he? And if I talk to him, he won't understand me?'

'No,' Toshev said, 'he won't understand you.'

'And if he talks to me, will I understand him?'

He tried to stand up, but the girl pulled him down.

'Don't go yet,' she said. 'Just a little longer.'

He let her keep her face on his chest, and listened to the beating of his own heart, which, he imagined, she too must be listening to. He tried to think of what he would do next week when his article was due. He thought of the Wallachians, of Ahmed and the shotgun. What if none of this was true? What if there were no Wallachians, just like there was no Greek couple?

Blindly, he caught the girl's chin and guided her up to his shoulder. Then he slid down and found her stomach and gathered away her skirt and lay his ear on it to listen. Her skin was warm against his face. He tried to imagine the baby, floating in complete darkness, unaware of its own existence, not even human-looking yet, but fish-like maybe, or like a lizard, devoid of a tangible form to weigh it down.

Up on the levee he had watched the frozen Danube, and far in the distance, on the water itself, he had noticed a tiny fire. The fire had flickered with the wind, and he'd understood that there, in the distance, the river wasn't completely solid ice. It had been, hours earlier, when someone had lit the fire to get some warmth and left it burning, and moved along. The river had broken through the ice and that fire, on a melting block, was floating to the sea. He had watched it drift farther away and wink out.

Now he felt terribly ashamed of himself, terribly guilty. He closed his eyes, and listened for a heartbeat, but all he heard was the girl's stomach grumbling, digesting what little goose she had eaten. With his finger he began to draw little lines on the girl's stomach, and, tickled, the girl laughed. Her laughter reminded him of the American woman, and before he knew it, the girl, the dark, the whole world were thick with that old smell, both frightening and reassuring. It hadn't been his fault back then, he told himself, and now again it wasn't.

His finger kept on tracing little lines, the emblem of the red car, he realized, an emblem which had etched itself in his mind forever. As would this shack, this girl, this awful fear, guilt, regret. Yet he didn't want this moment to pass, because after this moment there was an ugly tomorrow, when he would rise up and scurry away.

It's Ederlezi, Mama, he heard the girls singing. *It's St George's feast.*

The earth spun around him. The children from the orphanage were calling him Putty again. This was how the older kids tortured the young ones: they held his wrists and spun him around as hard as they could, until floor and ceiling and walls merged in a cacophonous centrifuge. Then they let go. And in that instant, before he went crashing into a chair, or a bed, or the wall even, in his flight, he was weightless. ■

WATER HAS NO ENEMY

Teju Cole

It is my first time back to Bar Beach, the most famous beach in Lagos, in almost twenty years. This was a place of weekend leisure for people of all classes when I was growing up, though my family did not visit it often, sometimes just once a year. It was also a place of violence, particularly during the years of military rule, the preferred spot for public executions at which alleged armed robbers, drug offenders and accused coup plotters were tied to wooden poles and shot before a gathered crowd in the early hours of the morning. These shootings – called 'the Bar Beach Show' – had a spiritual element to them: there were rumours some of the condemned had amulets that could protect them from bullets. The men of the firing squads were careful to remove these objects before taking up their positions. The most notorious armed robber of my childhood days, Lawrence 'The Law' Anini, a serial killer of police officers, was executed on Bar Beach in 1987. The beach was also a favoured gathering place for members of the aladura ('people of prayer') churches, particularly those affiliated with the Celestial Church of Christ. Aladuras wear white robes and practise a syncretic form of Christianity in which holy water and traditional beliefs about the sea play important roles. Their love of the sea was why Bar Beach was the setting of two of Soyinka's satirical plays about false prophets and gullible followers.

The white sands of Bar Beach extend a few miles on the southern edge of Victoria Island, alongside Ahmadu Bello Way. On the main road, self-appointed parking attendants harass visitors to the beach for tips, and riders on hungry-looking horses go back and forth along the boardwalk, eyeing tourist quarry. It is late in the afternoon on a Saturday in November. The sun glints off the white waves and

I can make out, in the far distance, a shimmering grey armada of container ships awaiting processing at Apapa Port and Tin Can Island. Closer to shore, there are high waves. I walk across the sand and see on the last large dune before the water a single red flag on a pole. Under the flag are two people, a man and a woman, at prayer. They finish just as I reach them. The man is changing his clothes and, caught at the moment in which the long satin robe he is wearing is arrested at his torso, its unfilled limbs flapping in the wind and catching the sunlight, he is like a pillar of fire. The woman's cotton dress is secured with a blue sash and her soft white cap sets off her black face against the sky. 'Mr Photographer, take our picture.' I oblige her with a few quick shots. 'So, how do we get these ones?' I ask if she has an email address. She answers with incredulous laughter, and says she thought I had a portable printer with me. The man finally fits into his robe, and takes up his bag and prayer bell. Compared to her plain cotton, the satin of his robe strikes an ostentatious note.

I leave them and continue on my way across the dune. A pair of riders approach me. Their horses move closer, I can see them coming, trudging slowly across the sand, but all of a sudden they are too close for comfort. 'Why you dey snap us?' At first I don't understand what he's saying. 'You dey snap us. Why you dey snap us?' He points to the camera slung around my neck. The horses circle, kicking up sand. The men, the one who has just spoken and the one who remains silent, look down at me. A danger has entered the afternoon. 'You no pay money, and you dey snap.' I gesture towards the horizon and, to show the requisite belligerence, say that it is no fault of mine if their horses enter the picture frame. They want money, and there is none to be had. The shadows of the pacing horses fall on me. Then the riders tire of the game, turn their horses around and ride away. I have been shooting them, and everything else that might be of interest: the sea, the shapes and angles and fast-moving light; I take pictures even though I know that Lagos is a difficult place in which to do public photography.

Less than five minutes pass before another man comes up to me, and this time there is no question of money. He is a fellow visitor to the beach. 'Why were you taking my picture?' he says in crisp English. 'I saw you pointing your camera at us.' I saw him when I crossed the dune, sitting with his girlfriend at some distance from the main crowds on the beach, but I hadn't taken any pictures of him, as I had guessed that he was on a date. I barely noticed them, and tell him so. 'Give me your camera. I want to review the pictures.' I have nothing to hide. All he'll see are photographs of horses, sand, sea and the aladura couple. But I detest the feeling of being commanded. Something in his vehemence makes me guess that the woman with him is someone with whom he doesn't wish to be publicly seen, a mistress perhaps. As we continue our dispute, an all-terrain vehicle roars past us, racing down the beach, keeping to the far line of the tide where the sand is most compacted. It has wide tyres and an open frame.

'Show-off,' the man says. 'Yes. They are the ones spoiling the country,' I add, eager to find common ground. The woman, who has been sitting during our argument, now comes up to where we are. She wears a red tank top which rises at the waist to reveal the tiny scoop of her navel. Other people have taken notice of the all-terrain vehicle now and have begun to jeer. She joins the jeers. Then, as we watch, the vehicle stops about three hundred metres from us, right at the edge of the shore. It is stuck. The driver revs it, but the compacted sand gives way, and the vehicle is mired deeper. By now, there is loud laughter all around the beach. Someone shouts, 'You see yourself?'

A big wave comes in, inundating man and car. He jumps out and grabs the iron frame of the vehicle and tries to pull it away from the ocean's edge. It won't budge. He struggles for a half-minute or so, frantic, to the sound of mocking voices. A second wave rams the shore and the man and his car both rise on the water and float. We can see that the man is still holding onto the car, still fighting to save it. Both are lifted and carried out on the receding wave. Laughter ceases. The driver lets go of the vehicle and the ocean swallows it. It's gone.

The man remains, and it becomes clear that he can't swim. He flails, fighting for his life. We watch and gasp, unable to help. Only after another big wave crests does a swimmer in black trunks race across the sand and dive in after him. The struggle is alarming but brief, and in less than a minute the diver drags a limp but still-living body out of the Atlantic and onto the shore. The vehicle has vanished without a trace, as though it was never even there.

Many more people have by now gathered from all over the beach, and the story is passed from those who have just seen it to those who have just missed it. A man hurrying past us on his way to a closer glimpse of the body says, 'Just ten minutes ago, a child was rescued on the other side of the beach, over there. He chased a ball into the water, and the divers brought him out,' and it's only as I listen to this that I remember my camera, which I have forgotten to use at all. From the distance, I take pictures of the man's prone body.

The Bar Beach crowd, buoyed by the story, takes on a carnivalesque character. An old trinket seller clambers across the dunes towards us. His manner is that of one intent on delivering a message, as though he were a chorus member in a play. When he reaches us, he clears his throat and begins a recitation in pidgin: 'Ocean no dey hear English. Ocean no dey hear Yoruba. Ocean no dey hear Igbo. Ocean no dey hear Edo. Ocean no dey hear Indian.' His eyes glisten, and there is a laconic irony in his manner. 'The thing wey ocean dey hear,' he says, pointing to the man lying on the shore. 'The thing wey ocean dey hear, him no fit talk.' Satisfied that he has delivered his message, he walks away from us, and away from the body, which is now being held into a sitting position and around which many more interested young men have gathered.

It is one thing to guess at the danger that is Lagos, quite another to experience it first-hand. Whenever I land at Murtala Muhammed International Airport – I go back once or twice each year – I feel that an actuary calculating my life-insurance premiums would have to temporarily charge me more. What I feel each time I enter the country is not a panic, exactly; it is rather a sense of fragility, of being more susceptible to accidents and incidents, as though some invisible veil of protection had been withdrawn, and fate, with all its hoarded hostility, could strike at any time. When I'm in the US, I argue with those who think Lagos is too dangerous a place to visit. I tell them I grew up there and wandered its streets for seventeen years, and nothing untoward happened to me. I point out that this is a city of 21 million people who wake up, brush their teeth, go to work, deal with hassles, sit in traffic, come home at night to eat dinner with their children and watch soap operas before going to bed and starting it all again the next day. There's modern infrastructure, there's entertainment, there's boredom; it isn't a battlefield. People in Lagos live normal lives in ordinary circumstances, just as people do in London and San Francisco and Jakarta.

I'm less defensive about Lagos when I'm actually there. After a few days back home, I begin to accumulate irritations and fears, and find that I am not alone in doing this. The city makes everyone tense and grouchy. One night, over beers and suya at a lounge in Ikoyi, my friends trade stories of close calls in the city. Some of them have been robbed, or have faced police brutality, or been forced, as I recently have, to pay a bribe. I commiserate with them, aware that most of them have no choice but to live there. I'm only a visitor, exposed to less of Lagos than they are, and I wonder at their tolerance for these numerous aggravations. How do they deal with it? Someone mentions the joys of family, and shows us pictures of his toddler and infant. Another says that vacations are key. 'I'm going to Italy soon for shopping and to spend time in a spa. That's what keeps me sane. I can't be in Lagos and have no upcoming vacations.' The others murmur their approval, though it's clear that not all could afford such a lavish stress-reduction programme. In the stories that are being told, we are all on one side of a contest, and Lagos, our adversary, the place we love to hate, is on the other.

My cousin Doyin and I leave the group around 8 p.m. Ikoyi is on the southern end of the city, not far from Victoria Island and about twenty miles from Ojodu, where my parents live. Fifteen years ago, Ojodu was still a sleepy and mostly forested northern suburb, but such has been the city's growth that now, not only is it fully enfolded in the city's life, it has in fact become one of the most congested neighbourhoods in all of Lagos, thick with sawmills, abattoirs, trailer parks and bus depots for the travellers to the north and east of Nigeria. The traffic in Ojodu can be a torment, but this is a Sunday, and the hour is late by Nigerian standards. We expect to be home within forty-five minutes. We clear most of Ikorodu Road, one of the main north–south arteries, easily, but things slow down at Ojota, where there is a major bus stop, and we come to a standstill. The windows of the jeep are rolled up, and we have the air conditioner going and the radio playing. While Doyin drives, I work on a small laptop with a mobile modem plugged into it. A street trader taps on the window on the driver's side. These boys are sometimes aggressive with their sales pitches, and we ignore this one. But he knocks more urgently and when I look up I see that he's waving a pistol. My momentary confusion is not dispelled by his pointing at my computer. His face is contorted with rage, and he's shouting. In the sealed interior of the jeep we can make out his words, 'I will shoot you! Wind down. I will shoot you!'

Even after I realize that we are being robbed, that bullets can shatter glass, that being locked in is no help in this situation, I still feel a vague resentment at having to hand the laptop over. It's mine. It contains my work, a week of writing, a month or more of photography, personal information. I have hesitated only a few seconds but feel as though I have just woken from a trance: briefly, I imagined myself with a bullet in my thigh, imagined myself bleeding out in traffic in Ojota. We turn the radio off and open the window. The gunman is small, thin-faced. We are surrounded by other cars but he doesn't stop shouting, as though something in him, and not he himself, were pushing the voice out of his chest. I don't even have the time to close my Facebook page or unplug the Internet modem. I close the laptop and hand it over to him. 'Your phones, your phones!

Give me your phones!' Doyin hands his BlackBerry over. I have to dig in my bag for the Nokia handset I use when I'm in Nigeria, my hands shaking the entire time. The man doesn't stop shouting. I've never had a loaded gun pointed at me before. Who is this man? What horrors of deprivation have pushed him to this extreme? His glare is so hard, so callous, that I am certain he doesn't see us, that he sees only whatever it is he imagines we represent.

In the unreal minutes after he leaves, I have the sensation of having drifted into an allegory of class warfare. We are still sitting at the same spot ten minutes later and we haven't stopped trembling. There are cars to the left and to the right, ahead and behind, but no one around us seems to have noticed anything. Finally the traffic eases, and we drive on towards Ojodu. I feel side-swiped, tired and violated in some basic existential way. I think again of my imaginary actuary, and how justified she might feel at this moment. Just two minutes' drive from where we were robbed, we see a group of heavily armed mobile police. Doyin and I look at each other and laugh. To report the crime to them would be a waste of time.

But half a mile from home, while we are still on the highway, the engine of the jeep stalls. Unable to start it again, we have to push it the rest of the way, with the unspoken fear that another gunman might show up. By the time we get to the house, my parents are frantic, demanding to know why we are so late and why we didn't call. When we tell them what has happened, my mother begins to weep. My other cousins are eager to tell stories of those they know who recently faced similar scenarios and were less lucky than we were: the friend who hesitated and was shot at but not hit, the co-worker who was hit and spent three months in hospital.

The city is a sea that can swallow you at any time, a monster that can lash out without warning, a hell of variables and uncertainties. What the solution should be is not clear. Would it be to refrain from using a laptop in traffic, or to avoid carrying a smartphone, or to have a loaded gun at the ready at all times?

I talk to Brother Jimoh at a raucous birthday and house-warming party during which the celebrant goes to a quiet corner of the house for a few minutes to beat his wife. Brother Jimoh, a short man with bulbous eyes, is one of the celebrant's best friends. The celebrant is a pensive fifty-year-old who doesn't seem the type to beat a woman in public or otherwise. Brother Jimoh is even more introverted, with a slight stammer and a cautious manner. His education was evidently interrupted at some point: the English is fluent but unpolished. We are in Ijebu Ode, an ancient town two hours north of Lagos, to which my friend Femi and I have come on dusty highways and back roads through old-growth rainforest.

Brother Jimoh tells me he's married but not currently with his wife. He lives in Lagos where he runs a hotel, but she lives in Japan and is in fact Japanese. He has only recently returned to Lagos from Nagoya, where he stayed for about twenty years and learned the language. His three children are half-Japanese, and he misses them. In his every word is a heavy regret. Then why did he leave? 'I had to come home,' he says. 'There's no place like home.' Drawn by the sensation of new possibilities, he joined the many flocking back to a democratic Nigeria. But he has not been able to convince his wife that Lagos is somewhere she can move to.

This is early on the day of the party. We are in the living room of the celebrant's new house, drinking tea. Brother Jimoh opens up his wallet and brings out pictures. His wife is a Japanese woman in her mid-forties, bright lipstick, straight bangs. The children are two teenagers and a pre-teen, their eyes are incongruous on their dark faces, and I think of Tiger Woods, but I think also about how we all look awkward in wallet pictures, how uncomfortable a photographer's studio is, especially when a parent is looking on. 'Very good children,' Brother Jimoh says, and for a moment he appears to be addressing them, and not me.

Brother Jimoh leaves the following day, driving one of the large and intimidating SUVs favoured by Nigeria's new elite. He looks small behind the wheel. He wears sunglasses, and waves goodbye.

After he leaves, I look up the hotel – it would be more accurate to call it a motel – which is in Mushin, one of the poorer neighbourhoods in Lagos. I can see that Brother Jimoh is catering to non-luxury customers. It is hard to find decent accommodation in Lagos, and in placing Nagoya City Hotel as he has in a working-class area some distance from Lagos Island, Brother Jimoh has hit on a formula that works. The website shows dowdy rooms, but the amenities listed (air conditioning, colour TV, DVD player, refrigerator) seem to promise enough comfort for modest spenders.

A few months later, I'm on the phone with Femi. We finish our conversation and he says, almost as an afterthought, 'You remember Brother Jimoh from the party?' Sure I do. 'It's a sad story,' Femi says. 'He was at his hotel, showing someone a gun he'd bought for security. You know how Lagos is. Anyway, I don't know what happened, but somehow it went off and he shot himself in the groin, and began to bleed. No one could help him. That was how the man died.'

Almost all of Lagos State is taken over by the city of Lagos, and the state capital, Ikeja, which was green and isolated when it was established, is now hectic like most other neighbourhoods in the city. I lived for many years in Ikeja as a boy, and it is to Ikeja that I go one morning, to a small, white two-storey building on a residential street. I have been given the address by my cousin Yemisi, who had called me in the US and said, 'Didn't you tell us a story last year about the man who almost drowned at Bar Beach? I found out that he goes to my church.' This man, whose name, she said, was Segun Odumosu, and whom I had expected never to hear of again, had stood up to give a public testimony of God's goodness to him. She was surprised to hear a story that matched the one I'd told her, but not as surprised as I was when she relayed it back to me. I made her promise to arrange a meeting.

The man who ushers me into his small, cool office on the second floor is in his mid-fifties, not twenty years younger as I expected. He runs his own business as a distributor of optical mark reader technology, better known to anyone who's taken multiple-choice exams in the US as Scantron. He prints and scans the papers, and maintains the machines for a number of public and private institutions in the country. Mr Odumosu is dark, slightly taller than average, with clear features, heavy-lidded eyes and a booming voice that one could imagine being, in different circumstances, jovial. He is a deeply intelligent man, with a serious but easy manner, and we talk about his love of jazz, his fourteen years of living in California (including a stint building nuclear power plants) until his return in the mid-eighties, and his political views: his immense distaste for the former dictators Babangida and Abacha, the awakening the writings of the Yoruba statesman Obafemi Awolowo spurred in him and his high opinion of the current Lagos State governor Babatunde Fashola.

To have seen a man at a distance and then to see him up close, alive and particular, robust with his own being in the world. He talks freely about the incident now. 'Almost nobody knew what happened to me, not till I got up to give a testimony at Daystar Christian Centre a year later. I kept it secret, probably out of shame. I got home that day – a commercial motorcyclist took me home because, somehow, the money hadn't fallen out of my pocket – and I just took a shower and sat in my bedroom in the dark.' After it happened, he told only a few people: his wife, his mechanic, his doctor. His wife because 'you can't hide things from women', his mechanic because the vehicle was miraculously recovered and he had to get it fixed, and his doctor because he had some chest pain afterwards and had to tell the truth. No one else knew: not his friends, not his children, not his other relatives. Then the anniversary of the incident arrived, and he felt he had a debt of gratitude that ought to be publicly acknowledged. The feeling of providential rescue was heightened for him by the fact that the date was significant.

'It was my birthday. I turned fifty-five that very day.' There was no party, just a few guests, all of whom had left by mid-afternoon. So, with his wife having gone to another party, he decided to go to the beach in his buggy (he refers always to his 'buggy', though I had assumed it was a conventional four-wheel-drive vehicle). Bar Beach is only a few miles away from his home in Lekki.

Mr Odumosu tells me he's long had an adventurous spirit. On a previous birthday, his fiftieth, his wife had taken him to Dubai. What she had in mind was a nice dinner at the Burj Al Arab, the expensive sailboat-shaped hotel. This did not interest him. 'As we were walking in the lobby, I saw a flyer for something called a Desert Safari, and I said, "Yes, this is it!" After two days of travel, I get tired of fancy food. But get me behind the wheel of a vehicle, put me on some sand dunes, and I'm as happy as can be. That's what I did for my birthday that time. So, on this day, it was the most natural thing to get in the buggy and go for a ride on the beach. I can't swim, but there's this friend of mine who often goes with me, and he's a good swimmer. So I never even thought of the possibility of anything happening. That day, he wasn't around, so I went by myself.'

One would suppose that something like one in every 365 people die on their birthdays, but statistical studies suggest an even greater frequency. This was the fate that befell Constantine Cavafy, Sidney Bechet and Ingrid Bergman, among countless others; tradition says that it is also true of Moses, King David, the prophet Muhammad and Shakespeare. 'That the first day should make the last, that the Tail of the Snake should return into its Mouth precisely at that time, and they should wind up upon the day of their Nativity, is indeed a remarkable Coincidence,' wrote Sir Thomas Browne in the seventeenth century, in eerie anticipation of the fate which was also to be his own.

'I saw you that day,' I tell Mr Odumosu. 'On your birthday. I watched the whole thing. I thought I was watching a man die.'

'Something told me it wasn't my time. I wouldn't say I was scared,' he says. 'When the water pulled me in, I realized something was going on. I became concerned. Scared was not the word. Concerned. Very, very concerned. Like, what's going on here? I thought, "I can't just die like this." Something told me very clearly it just wasn't my time to go yet.'

'The vehicle sank, and you began to disappear too. We began to lose sight of you. That's when the other man dived in.'

'That's when I suddenly heard a voice saying, "Take my hand, take my hand!" And I thought, "I'm not taking your hand, man, I'm grabbing your waist!" Because I'm much bigger than him, and I knew if I took his hand, it could slip. So I just held on to his waist.'

At moments, Mr Odumosu is silent, clearly still full of a belated alarm. He tells me about the man who saved him. His name is Peter and he's from Kaduna, in the northern part of the country, though he's a Christian. He's in his late twenties or early thirties, and works in a laundry. 'I wasn't the first person he had saved that day. Apparently he had dragged some other person out earlier in the day. He hangs around the beach, and he's a good swimmer. So, you see, when I say it wasn't my time, that's what I mean. The guy's name is Peter. What does that mean? "Fisher of men". And I told him this later, that God had a special purpose for him. Such a humble and unassuming fellow. I consider him my brother now. More than a friend. God bound us together. He asked me for nothing, unlike the others.'

'Other guys?'

'When I went back to the beach the next day, some guys had retrieved the buggy – Peter had called me to say they had brought it out of the water – and of course they wanted money. I wanted to pay one guy with whatever little amount I had on me, but they referred me to their head guy on the beach, the guy I was supposed to negotiate with. His name is Water, they said. Water was what they called him, and like the Fela song, "Water No Get Enemy", they said, he has no enemy. And I was joking about my predicament, and said, "This water was rough yesterday to me, this one was my enemy. In fact I shouldn't have to pay money today."'

For weeks afterwards, the gloom of his narrow escape and the solitude of keeping it to himself altered his way of being in the world. 'When I would be in a meeting or among people who were arguing about something, I would just think to myself, "What's the big deal? I'm not even supposed to be here, so what's the big deal? I shouldn't be here." But then the depression lifted. Life goes on.'

The marine geography of Lagos is complex. The city sits on the coast, facing the Atlantic Ocean, but water infiltrates the land in the form of a large lagoon, and through many creeks, swamps, rivers and lakes. These calm waters were to Lagos's great advantage in the eighteenth and nineteenth centuries as a slave market. The city remains one of the largest and busiest ports in Africa. The quieter waters are also the playground of the rich in their speedboats and yachts, and a notable marker of prestige in present-day Lagos is membership at the Lagos Motor Boat Club. The club is located in Ikoyi, in a white colonial-era building that looks out on Five Cowrie Creek on which docked boats bob. The view is especially fine on clear evenings, and on one such evening I visit the club for a concert by Hugh Masekela. The attendees are a mix of the insouciantly wealthy, both Nigerian and expatriate, and those who are enamoured enough of jazz to pay the N14,000 (about $100) entry fee. I am at the concert with Pierre, a European banker who only arrived to work in Nigeria two days before, and on whose face I can see the daze that comes over those who are thrown into Lagos life without preparation. Drinks and food are served, and Masekela's trumpet traces an arc across the night air over the creek with a music so full of warmth and experience that it is like lucid dreaming. The atmosphere is exuberant, and becomes more and more so until loud talkers drown out the music. Masekela jokes good-naturedly about noisy Nigerians, and asks people to quiet down, but then he brings the house to its feet with a raucous cover of Fela's 'Lady'.

Even here, among the badly behaved rich, not far from the poverty and desperation of the streets beyond the boathouse, even here where I notice a limit to free-spiritedness when a man dancing in front of us gently removes his male partner's hand from his waist, even here with my cascade of doubts and second thoughts, I still feel that this is Lagos at its best: good food, great music, people dancing and a sensational vista. A costly joy is a joy nonetheless. I am talking to Pierre during a break in the music when a man passes by us with a drink in his hand. He has a faraway look about him, and when we catch each other's eyes, he frowns and says, 'Haven't we met?' It is Mr Odumosu, the man who was saved from the sea. We say a quick hello. This is about a year after I last spoke to him, and he is somewhat elusive, distracted, as though lofted by something unseen towards something unknown, like the notes that Masekela begins once again to send out across the darkness and over the water. ■

© TEJU COLE

Questions of Travel by *Michelle de Kretser*

'This is a novel unlike any other I have read . . . It is not really possible to describe the originality and depth of this long and beautifully crafted book.' A.S. Byatt, *Guardian*

Laura travels the world before returning to Sydney. Ravi dreams of being a tourist until he is forced to flee Sri Lanka. Through these two superbly drawn characters, Michelle de Kretser illuminates travel, work and modern dreams.

Allen & Unwin £12.99 | **HB**

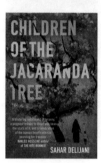

Children of the Jacaranda Tree by *Sahar Delijani*

'Set in post-revolutionary Iran, Delijani's gripping novel is a blistering indictment of tyranny, a poignant tribute to those who bear the scars of it and a celebration of the human's heart's eternal yearning for freedom.' Khaled Hosseini

A powerful debut novel about the ghosts of revolution and forging the future when your past is too painful to remember.

Weidenfeld & Nicolson £12.99 | **HB**

Travels in China by *Roland Barthes*

'The book's most charming aspect is his little sketches: of hairstyles, or statues, or seating plans, and one tiny caricature of a near-featureless but somehow reassuring Confucius, an apparition perhaps of one whom Barthes wished to meet but didn't.' *Guardian*

'An image of pre-capitalist China, a snapshot of a nation that has changed utterly in the past thirty-five years.' *Sydney Morning Herald*

Polity Press £12.99 | **PB**

Traveling in Place: A History of Armchair Travel by *Bernd Stiegler*

'Bernd Stiegler shows the degree to which the room of the writer has become a microcosm, already stocked with enough exotic detail to place itself at the infinite disposal of our curiosity. The book suggests that, no matter how far any wandering sightseer might travel, what really embarks upon the trek is our imagination.' Christian Bök, author of *Euonia*. Forthcoming in November. Available for pre-order.

University of Chicago Press £17.50 | **HB**

The Society of Authors

Authors' Foundation grants and awards

K Blundell Trust awards
(open to writers under 40 years of age)

Next closing dates –
September 30 2013
and **April 30 2014**

Full guidelines
available from
www.societyofauthors.org
020 7373 6642

The Royal Literary Fund

FINANCIAL ASSISTANCE FOR WRITERS

The Royal Literary Fund (est.1790) helps published
authors in financial difficulties. Last year it awarded
grants and pensions to over 200 writers.
Applications are welcome throughout the year.

For more information contact:
Eileen Gunn | Chief Executive
The Royal Literary Fund
3 Johnson's Court | London EC4A 3EA
Tel: 020 7353 7159
email: egunnrlf@globalnet.co.uk
www.rlf.org.uk
Registered Charity no 219952Tel 020 7353 7159
email: egunnrlf@globalnet.co.uk
website: www.rlf.org.uk
Registered Charity No. 219952

EDITORIAL
- Detailed critical assessments and services by professional editors for writing at all stages of development, in all genres
- Links with publishers and agents, and advice on self-publishing

MENTORING
- Six online one-to-one sessions with a professional editor
- Includes separate manuscript assessment and industry day with publishers and agents

EVENTS
- Writing in a Digital Age: two-day summer conference
- Masterclasses and skills workshops
- Literary events and overseas writing retreat

TLC The Literary Consultancy
Literary Values in a Digital Age

T 020 7324 2563
E info@literaryconsultancy.co.uk
W www.literaryconsultancy.co.uk

Supported using public funding by
ARTS COUNCIL ENGLAND

CONTRIBUTORS

Héctor Abad is a Colombian writer and journalist born in Medellín. His books in English translation include *Oblivion: A Memoir* and *Recipes for Sad Women.*

Eric Abrahamsen is a translator and publishing consultant who has lived in China since 2001. He is the recipient of PEN and National Endowment for the Arts translation grants. His most recent translation is *The Civil Servant's Notebook* by Wang Xiaofang.

Archive of Modern Conflict is a photo archive and publisher based in London. Their journal, *AMC2*, and other publications can be seen at amcbooks.com.

Rachael Boast's *Sidereal* won the Forward Prize for Best First Collection and the Seamus Heaney Centre for Poetry Prize. 'Compass Plant' is taken from *Pilgrim's Flower*, forthcoming from Picador in October.

Teju Cole is Distinguished Writer in Residence at Bard College. His most recent book, *Open City*, won the 2012 PEN/ Hemingway Foundation Award.

Dave Eggers is the author of seven books, most recently *A Hologram for the King.* He is founder and editor of McSweeney's, an independent publisher based in San Francisco, and co-founder of 826 Valencia, a non-profit writing and tutoring centre for youth.

Sonia Faleiro is the author of *Beautiful Thing: Inside the Secret World of Bombay's Dance Bars.* She is a frequent contributor to the *New York Times.*

Philip Gabriel is professor of Japanese literature at the University of Arizona. He has translated four novels, two works of non-fiction and various short stories by Haruki Murakami. His most recent translations are Book 3 of Murakami's *1Q84* and the novel *Villain*, by Shuichi Yoshida.

Phil Klay is a Marine Corps veteran of Operation Iraqi Freedom and a graduate of the MFA programme at Hunter College. He is a contributor to *Fire and Forget: Short Stories from the Long War* and the author of the forthcoming story collection *Redeployment.*

Steffi Klenz is a German artist living in London. Her work has been exhibited at the Royal Academy of Arts in London and Künstlerhaus Bethanien in Berlin, among others. Her monograph, *Polo Bound for Passaic*, was published in 2009.

Rattawut Lapcharoensap is the author of *Sightseeing*, a collection of short stories. He lives in Wyoming.

Robert Macfarlane is the author of *Mountains of the Mind, The Wild Places* and, most recently, *The Old Ways.* He is at work on *Underland*, a book about subterranea and the lost worlds beneath our feet. He is a Fellow of Emmanuel College, Cambridge.

Anne McLean translates novels, short stories, memoirs, travelogues and other writings by authors including Héctor Abad, Javier Cercas and Julio Cortázar.

Siddhartha Mukherjee is a physician, scientist and writer. His book, *The Emperor of All Maladies: A Biography of Cancer*, won the 2011 Pulitzer Prize. He is currently an assistant professor of medicine at Columbia University in New York.

Haruki Murakami's work has been translated into more than forty languages. He is the recipient of a host of international awards including the Franz Kafka Prize and the Jerusalem Prize.

Miroslav Penkov was born and raised in Bulgaria. He is the author of the story collection *East of the West* and teaches at the University of North Texas, where he is a fiction editor for *American Literary Review*.

David Searcy lives in Dallas, Texas. His first collection of essays, *Shame and Wonder*, is published in 2014.

Charles Simic's *New and Selected Poems: 1962–2012* was published in March. He divides his time between New York City and a small town in New Hampshire.

Saskia Vogel is a translator from Swedish and German and the publicist at *Granta*. Her stories have appeared in *The White Review*, *The Erotic Review* and *Zocalo Public Square*. She is currently completing a novel with the working title *I Am a Pornographer*.

Ellen Bryant Voigt has published seven volumes of poetry, including *Kyrie*, a National Book Critics Circle Award finalist; *Shadow of Heaven*, a National Book Award finalist; and *Messenger: New and Selected Poems 1976–2006*, winner of the Poets' Prize and a finalist for both the National Book Award and the Pulitzer Prize. 'Geese' is taken from a new collection of poems, *Headwaters*, published in October by W.W. Norton.

Lina Wolff is the author of the story collection *Många människor dör som du* (*Many People Die Like You*). In 2012, she was awarded *Vi* magazine's prize for literature for her novel *Bret Easton Ellis och de andra hundarna* (*Bret Easton Ellis and the Other Dogs*). She lives in southern Sweden.

Samantha Wynne-Rhydderch's third collection, *Banjo*, was shortlisted for the Wales Book of the Year Award. 'String Theory' is taken from her pamphlet, *Lime & Winter*, published in 2014 by Rack Press.

A Yi's works in Chinese include two novels, *Now, What Shall I Do Next?* and *Where Is Spring*, and two story collections, *Grey Stories* and *The Bird Saw Me*.

GRANTA 124: TRAVEL

CALENDAR OF EVENTS

Celebrate the launch of *Granta* 124: Travel with readings, conversation and drinks with contributors and *Granta* editors. All events are open to the public. Please visit granta.com/events for further details and updates.

The San Francisco Launch

16 July, 7 p.m., Green Apple Books, 506 Clement Street, San Francisco, CA 94118. Free.

The London Launch

17 July, 6.30 p.m., Foyles, 113 – 119 Charing Cross Road, London WC2H 0EB. £3. Please book via foyles.co.uk/events.

The New York Launch

24 July, 7 p.m., Bookcourt, 163 Court Street, Brooklyn, NY 11201. Free.

Liars' League Presents Granta 124: Travel

16 July, doors at 6.30 p.m., event at 7 p.m., The Betsey Trotwood, 56 Farringdon Road, London EC1R 3BL. £7, tickets include a copy of Granta 124. Tickets are only available at the door. RSVP to events@granta.com to reserve your place.

The Best of Young British Novelists World Tour

continues with events coming up at Latitude Festival in Southwold, UK (18 July), Hendrick's Carnival of Knowledge in Edinburgh (9 August), Edinburgh International Book Festival (10 to 26 August), Small Wonder Festival in Charleston, UK (26 to 29 September), and further events in partnership with the British Council in Moscow, Sussex and beyond.

The Granta Literary Salon

10 July, 7 p.m., New York University Paris, 56 rue de Passy, 75016 Paris, France. Seating is limited and RSVPs are required: nyucwp.rsvp@gmail.com.